in the
kitchen
with DAVID®

QVC's Resident Foodie Presents

Half Homemade,
Fully Delicious

DAVID VENABLE
Foreword by Geoffrey Zakarian

BALLANTINE BOOKS | NEW YORK

Published in the United States by Ballantine Books, an imprint of Random House, a division of Penguin Random House LLC, New York

BALLANTINE and the HOUSE colophon are registered trademarks of Penguin Random House LLC.

Hardback ISBN 978-0-593-35796-5
Ebook ISBN 978-0-593-35797-2

Printed in the United States of America on acid-free paper

randomhousebooks.com

2 4 6 8 9 7 5 3 1

First Edition

Book design by Ana Tamaccio, Gregory McDonnell, and Kelcey Hurst

For dedicated home cooks working to put balanced meals together in record time

CONTENTS

FOREWORD

When I first met David Venable at the 2019 housewares show in Chicago, I could immediately tell that he is truly a one-of-a-kind gentleman and knew that I wanted to work with him.

David's energy on and off camera is infectious and genuine. His passion for food and his knowledge on elevating the home-cooking and kitchen experience translate seamlessly through his show, *In the Kitchen with David,* on QVC. For those of you who don't know David personally, I can assure you that he is as authentic as they come. (He's also one of the funniest people I know.) It is an honor to call David a friend on and off camera.

David understands how busy life can get and that we often don't have the time to make the kind of comforting food we all want and need. He knows the important role food plays in bringing joy into your home and how the act of sharing a meal with friends and family helps strengthen relationships.

David's mission is to share the kinds of recipes that deliver layers of flavor along with satisfying textures that even the busiest of us can make quickly and easily, and still get rave reviews.

As a chef, I've spent years perfecting dishes in restaurant kitchens, creating products for QVC that simplify life for the busiest home cooks, and competing against the clock on TV cooking competitions. With three kids and a full work schedule, I know more than ever the value of spending less time at the stove and more time around the table.

What David does better than anyone that I know is take the simplest, most ordinary ingredients and, in practically no time, create something extraordinary. In this book, *Half Homemade, Fully Delicious,* David shares his secrets on how to make incredible meals incredibly easy. He expertly shows you how to take store-bought staples and pair them with fresh ingredients for dishes that never compromise on taste.

For something a little out of the ordinary, try his Chicken Tagine made in a Dutch oven. Or his gorgeous and hearty Steak Caesar Salad with charred onions and a creamy blue cheese dressing. It's perfect for a weeknight meal or your weekend dinner guests. Moist Oat-Banana Pancakes with Peanut Butter Syrup is an updated breakfast classic that is destined to become a Zakarian family favorite. It'll become one in your home, too.

What David has done in *Half Homemade, Fully Delicious* is serve up a collection of recipes that are the perfect combination of time-tested classics with a twist and completely new creations that always deliver "yums" and smiles when brought to the table. And the best part is how quickly you can make them using supermarket shortcuts of prepped vegetables, canned beans, and jars of sauces.

My favorite cookbooks are those that have pages stained from years of repeated use with recipes that are the perfect balance of tried-and-true favorites and exciting ingredients that always deliver. If you're looking for easy chef-approved recipes that you can trust, David's book checks all of those boxes! Once you have a copy of *Half Homemade, Fully Delicious* in your hands, I know that you will reach for it again and again through the years, as many of David's recipes become your family's favorites.

From someone who has spent his professional life working in kitchens and reading through cookbooks, David Venable's *Half Homemade, Fully Delicious* is a rare find that you'll treasure for years to come.

IRON CHEF
GEOFFREY ZAKARIAN

INTRODUCTION

Oh. My. Word.

How did our lives become so busy? If your calendar looks anything like mine, then you know how those hours, days, and weeks seem to have become shorter and shorter. Because we have so many work, family, and other obligations, we need to make choices about how we want to spend these precious moments.

As you know from our twice-weekly visits on *In the Kitchen with David* on QVC, I love to cook. I love to eat. (Cue my happy dance!) I love everything about cooking except dicing piles of onions, carrots, and celery and measuring spices to make the perfect seasoning blend. If there are ways to take the "work" out of prep work, count me in.

Well, there's good news, foodie friends. *Half Homemade, Fully Delicious* is loaded with creative ideas for getting great comfort food on the table while spending far less time in the kitchen. All of the 110 recipes in my newest collection use ten ingredients or fewer. Most of them take advantage of "supermarket short-cuts," those handy, ready-to-use products from every aisle in the grocery store that will streamline your cooking. By using these culinary quick tricks to your advantage, you'll reach your destination—the dining table—in a fraction of the time it traditionally takes to prepare meals, all without sacrificing the flavors and texture of your favorite dishes.

Before supermarket shortcuts, making dishes like Butternut Squash Hummus (page 13) would have meant peeling, seeding, and cutting up the squash; soaking and cooking dried chickpeas; and toasting and puréeing sesame seeds. Now, all I have to do is roast some already prepped squash pieces, then combine them with a can of chickpeas and some jarred tahini. On every grocery run, I pick up a rotisserie chicken or two knowing that over the course of the week, I will use them along with other readily available ingredients.

For the Barbecue Chicken Salad (page 72), the meat is tossed with bottled barbecue sauce and ranch dressing, then combined with lettuce and canned black beans and corn. Shredded chicken from one bird goes into a pot along with cubed vegetables, boxed chicken stock, frozen peas and carrots, and canned cream of chicken soup for a warming Creamy Chicken Pot Pie Soup with Dippers (page 46). Oh, and it's ready to be ladled into bowls in less than thirty minutes. Now, that's quick and easy.

Having these ready-to-use ingredients at my fingertips inspires me to re-create new versions of memorable, comforting dishes from my childhood, travels, restaurants I've eaten in, and meals I've enjoyed at the homes of friends. The time needed to make D-I-Y Deviled Eggs (page 18), a must-have at every Southern gathering, is minimal when you use already hard-boiled-and-peeled eggs. Buying the cooked eggs allows you to spend more time on inventive toppings. The Reuben "Sandwich" Skillet Bake (page 159) is a variation on my favorite deli sandwich and takes advantage of frozen hash browns, canned sauerkraut, corned beef from the deli, and Thousand Island dressing. (Think about the time you would have to spend to make just one of those ingredients from scratch.) Trips to our fiftieth state sparked me to combine canned pineapple, already-cooked ham steak, and Original Hawaiian Sweet Rolls in the Hawaiian Breakfast Bake (page 26). When I first started out on local television, I relied on inexpensive and filling ramen noodle packets. Those packets gave me the idea for my Beef Ramen Bowls (page 96), a dish much improved with skirt steak, mushrooms, and General Tso's sauce. Turtle Brookies (page 169) use a box of brownie mix and a bag of chocolate chip cookie mix for a best-of-both-worlds dessert.

The beauty of these recipes is how much room they give you to make them your own. If you like more heat, add some extra chopped jalapeño to Creamy Corn off the Cob (page 179). For additional tang, use a tad more vinegar in the Greek Salad (page 63).

You'll love how much time you can save by mixing and matching ingredients from the store's many aisles and departments. Southwestern Skillet Scampi (page 127) uses fresh tomato salsa from the refrigerator section, shrimp from the freezer section, and black beans and diced green chiles from the canned goods aisle. I love the Chicken, Broccoli, and Rice Casserole (page 142), a dish of my mom's that I fondly remember. Just use a rotisserie chicken, a box of broth, frozen broccoli florets, a can of cream of broccoli soup, and a package of precooked rice. These dishes come together in no time with supermarket shortcuts.

To make things even easier, many of these recipes not only can be made ahead, but they can also be frozen. Just heat and serve when you need it. Talk about food fast with a wow factor!

With supermarket shortcuts and my new collection of comfort recipes in *Half Homemade, Fully Delicious,* you'll rediscover the pleasures of sharing meals and good times. No matter how busy you get, you can always find the time to make food that'll get you "oohs" and "aaahs." Only you will know how quickly you got it done.

Let's get started.

DAVID'S
SUPERMARKET
SHORTCUTS

Throughout *Half Homemade, Fully Delicious*, many of the ingredients listed in the recipes appear in **bold.** From pound cake mix to pumpkin purée and refrigerated biscuits to ranch dressing, these highlighted supermarket shortcuts cut down your prep work and cooking times while adding layers of flavors and textures to the finished dishes. Here's an easy-to-use guide to make your grocery shopping easier. Time saved in the kitchen means time spent doing other things you love and with those you love.

CANS AND JARS, BOXES AND BAGS

Alfredo sauce

Baby corn

Beans: black, kidney, pinto, refried, and small white

Black olives, sliced

Capers

Caramel syrup

Cheez Whiz Original Cheese Dip

Chickpeas

Chipotle peppers in adobo

Coconut milk (full fat)

Corn kernels

Cream of broccoli soup

Cream of chicken soup

Cream of shrimp soup

Cream Style Sweet Corn

Crispy fried onions

Diced green chiles

Diced tomatoes with basil, garlic, and oregano

Dried cranberries

Dried sliced peaches

Dulce de leche

Fig jam

Four fruits preserves

Fruit cocktail in syrup

Instant espresso coffee granules

Italian mix giardiniera

Low-sodium beef, chicken, and vegetable broths

Mandarin orange segments

Maraschino cherries

Marinara sauce

Marshmallow crème

Mild chili

Orange marmalade

Peach preserves

Pear halves in syrup

Pepperoncini

Pesto

Petite diced tomatoes

Pineapple: chunks, crushed, slices, and juice

Pizza sauce

Potato sticks

Pumpkin purée

Quick-cooking grits

Ramen noodle packages

Red enchilada sauce

Roasted red peppers

RO*TEL Diced Tomatoes and Green Chilies

Sauerkraut

Sea salt chickpeas

Seedless raspberry jam

Sloppy joe sauce

Strawberry jam

Sun-dried tomato pesto

Sugar-free, fat-free cheesecake flavor instant pudding mix

Taco sauce

Tomato sauce

Tomato soup

Tuna, packed in water

Velveeta

Water chestnuts, diced

Whipped cream

White chocolate instant pudding mix

Whole baby clams

Worcestershire sauce

PRODUCE

Baby-cut carrots

Bell peppers, cored, seeded,
and cubed or sliced

Butternut squash, peeled and cubed

Celery, sliced or chopped

Mirepoix (diced celery, onion, and carrot)

Red and yellow onions, chopped or sliced

Seedless watermelon slices

Shredded iceberg lettuce

Sliced baby bella and white mushrooms

Sweet potatoes, peeled
and cut into chunks

BREADS, CEREALS, PASTA, AND RICE

Ben's Original Ready Rice

Bread crumbs: Italian seasoned
and plain

Croutons

Granola

New Orleans Style Fish Fry Seafood
Breading Mix

Original Hawaiian Sweet Rolls

Oreo Pie Crust

Ritz crackers

BAKING

Bisquick

Brownie mix

Candied pecans

Chocolate chip cookie mix

Chocolate shavings

Glazed donuts

Just-add-water
pancake/waffle mix

Lotus Biscoff cookies

Pound cake mix

Spice cake mix

Sweetened shredded coconut

PREPARED FOODS

Cooked carved turkey breast

Precooked ham steak

Rotisserie chicken

Sandwich-sliced corned beef

Sliced cooked chicken breast

FROZEN FOODS

Asian stir-fry vegetable blend

Broccoli florets

Chopped peppers and onions

Chopped spinach

Classic mixed vegetables

Cool Whip

Corn kernels

Cranberries

Fire-roasted diced red bell peppers

Freeze-dried chives

Mango chunks and pulp

Mixed frozen sliced berries

Pearl onions

Peas

Peas and carrots

Potatoes: O'Brien with onions and peppers, diced hash browns, shredded hash browns, and wedges

Shrimp

Tater Tots

REFRIGERATED FOODS

Blue cheese crumbles

Cinnamon rolls with icing

Cooked lobster

Crescent rolls

Diced pancetta

Egg roll wrappers

Feta crumbles

Fresh shaved beef

Fresh tomato salsa

Garlic-and-herbs spreadable cheese

Goat cheese crumbles

Gorgonzola crumbles

Hard-boiled and peeled eggs

Mozzarella: shredded whole-milk and part-skim, low-moisture

Olives, kalamata and green, pitted

Parmigiano-Reggiano shavings

Pepperoni Minis

Pie crust

Pillsbury Grands! Southern Homestyle Original biscuits

Pimiento cheese spread

Sharp Cheddar cheese spread

Sliced prosciutto

Tzatziki

CONDIMENTS AND DRESSINGS

Barbecue sauce
Blue cheese dressing
Buffalo wing sauce
Chili sauce
Chocolate sauce
Coleslaw dressing
Dill pickle relish
Dill pickles
Duck sauce
General Tso's sauce
Hoisin sauce
Honey Mustard
Honeyracha Saucy Sauce

Horseradish
Horseradish sauce
Hot sauce
Mayoracha Saucy Sauce
Mild wet jerk seasoning
Mojo criollo marinade
Ranch dressing
Steak sauce
Sweet chili sauce
Tahini
Thick teriyaki sauce
Thousand Island dressing
Turkey gravy

DRY SEASONINGS AND SPICES

Balsamic dressing & recipe mix
Brown gravy mix
Cajun seasoning
Chicken-flavor bouillon cubes
Country gravy mix
Creole seasoning
Dry barbecue rub
Everything-but-the-bagel seasoning
Fajita seasoning mix
Five-spice powder
Gingerbread spice
Italian salad dressing & recipe mix
Italian seasoning

Lawry's Seasoned Salt
McCormick Grill Mates Roasted
Garlic & Herb Seasoning
Old Bay Seasoning
Onion soup & dip mix
Pumpkin pie spice
Ranch seasoning &
salad dressing mix
Ras el hanout spice blend
Sloppy joe seasoning mix
Stir-fry seasoning mix
Vegetable Magic seasoning blend

APPETIZERS:

GRAND OPENINGS

When guests walk into your home for the evening, set the stage with welcoming appetizers. Offer them just a few satisfying bites along with a glass of wine or your house cocktail. That way your friends and family will have plenty of room left to enjoy the main meal when it's time to sit down at the table. Most of these appetizers take full advantage of supermarket shortcuts. Southwestern-inspired Tex-Mex Egg Rolls with shaved beef, frozen chopped vegetables, and two jarred sauces are assembled well ahead of time and finished just before your guests ring the bell. Butternut Squash Hummus uses already peeled and cubed squash along with canned chickpeas and jarred tahini. For the not-your-grandma's D-I-Y Deviled Eggs, you can buy already hard-boiled and peeled eggs and spend your time on the eye-popping toppings. If time is short, wow your guests with a Nibble Board, composed entirely of sliced deli meats, cheeses, marinated or fresh vegetables, dried fruit, nuts, and breadsticks—you name it.

Tex-Mex Egg Rolls

Dunk one of these Southwestern-inspired rolls into the zesty dipping sauce. Take a bite. You won't believe how much deliciousness is packed into one appetizer. The crispy wrapper, gooey cheese, beefy filling, and peppery cilantro all come together for an explosion of textures and flavors.

MAKES 10

¾ cup plus ¼ cup **taco sauce**

¼ cup **Mayoracha Saucy Sauce**

2 teaspoons vegetable oil, plus more for deep-frying

1 14-ounce package **fresh shaved beef**

¾ teaspoon garlic salt

¾ teaspoon freshly ground black pepper

1 cup **frozen chopped peppers and onions**

¼ cup chopped fresh cilantro leaves

10 **egg roll wrappers**

12 ounces **Velveeta**, cut into 1-inch pieces

Whisk together ¾ cup taco sauce and the Mayoracha sauce in a bowl. Set aside.

Heat 2 teaspoons oil in a skillet over medium-high heat. Add the beef, garlic salt, and pepper. Cook, stirring occasionally to break up the beef into smaller pieces, until the meat is cooked through and no longer pink, 4 to 5 minutes. Put the cooked beef in a bowl, leaving any juices in the skillet. Add the peppers and onions to the skillet and cook, stirring occasionally, until they are tender, 2 to 3 minutes. Stir the vegetables, the remaining ¼ cup taco sauce, and the cilantro into the bowl with the beef.

Position 1 wrapper on a work surface like a diamond. Place 3 tablespoons of the beef mixture and 2 cheese cubes on the corner nearest you and spread it up the middle. Using a pastry brush, brush the edges with a little water. Fold the nearest corner up over the mixture, then fold the left and right corners toward the center and continue to roll. Brush the final corner with water to seal. Repeat with the remaining wrappers, cheese, and beef mixture.

Clip a deep-frying thermometer to the side of a deep pot. Add 2 inches of oil and slowly heat it to 350°F. Working in batches to avoid overcrowding, add the egg rolls and cook until golden brown, 3 to 5 minutes. Drain on paper towels. Serve hot with the sauce.

Cheeseburger Hand Pies

Cheeseburgers are the classic American sandwich. All the beefy, cheesy goodness is captured in these handy hand pies. This treat is not complete without a dipping sauce. Mine is an easy blend of favorite toppings—mayonnaise, mustard, ketchup, and relish.

MAKES 8 SERVINGS

8 ounces lean ground beef

½ teaspoon kosher salt

3 tablespoons plus 6 tablespoons **pickle relish**

3 tablespoons plus 6 tablespoons ketchup

2 tablespoons plus 1 tablespoon mustard

6 slices American cheese, finely chopped

1 14-ounce package **refrigerated pie crust**, at room temperature

1 large egg, beaten

1 tablespoon sesame seeds

⅓ cup mayonnaise

Heat the oven to 400°F. Line a sheet pan with parchment paper.

Put the beef and salt in a skillet over medium heat. Sauté the meat, breaking it up with a spoon, until it is browned and crumbled, 4 to 5 minutes. Remove the meat to a bowl and discard any fat in the skillet. Stir 3 tablespoons pickle relish, 3 tablespoons ketchup, and 2 tablespoons mustard into the meat. Mix in the cheese. Let cool.

Unroll the pie crusts. Cut each one into 4 triangles. Spoon about 3 tablespoons of the beef mixture into the center of each triangle. Brush the edges of the pastry with the beaten egg. Fold each in half to create a triangle pocket, then tightly press and seal the edges with a fork.

Arrange the hand pies on the prepared pan. Brush the top of each hand pie with the beaten egg. Sprinkle with the sesame seeds. Bake until golden brown, 20 to 22 minutes.

While the hand pies are baking, whisk together the mayonnaise and the remaining 6 tablespoons relish, 6 tablespoons ketchup, and 1 tablespoon mustard in a bowl. Serve the sauce with the warm hand pies.

Bacon-Wrapped Chicken Bites with Barbecue Dipping Sauce

Pieces of boneless chicken breast are dusted with ranch seasoning, then wrapped in bacon and given a second sprinkling of ranch. Air-frying these appetizers is the only way to get that crispiness we all love. Whisk together some sour cream, barbecue sauce, and a bit more ranch seasoning for dipping.

MAKES 20

½ cup sour cream

¼ cup bottled **barbecue sauce**

1 tablespoon plus ½ cup plus 1 teaspoon **ranch seasoning & salad dressing mix**

¼ teaspoon plus ½ teaspoon freshly ground black pepper

1½ pounds boneless, skinless chicken breast, cut into 1-inch pieces

10 bacon slices, halved

Vegetable oil spray

Whisk together the sour cream, barbecue sauce, 1 tablespoon ranch seasoning mix, and ¼ teaspoon pepper in a bowl. Set the sauce aside.

Place ½ cup ranch seasoning mix and the chicken pieces in a bowl and toss to coat. Wrap each chicken piece in bacon and secure with a toothpick. Sprinkle the remaining 1 teaspoon ranch seasoning mix and ½ teaspoon pepper on the wrapped chicken pieces.

Set the air fryer to 400°F. Spray the frying basket with vegetable oil spray. Put the chicken bites in the frying basket and cook until the bacon is crisp and the chicken is cooked through, 23 to 28 minutes. Shake the basket 2 or 3 times while air-frying. Serve hot with the dipping sauce.

Baked Brie in a Bread Bowl

Trust me, everyone is going to ask you for this recipe after the first bite. Hollow out a round bread and save the bread chunks to toast for dipping. Spread fig jam on the inside, then nestle a Brie wheel in the center and top with another layer of jam. The entire "dish" is baked and served right out of the oven. Once your guests devour the toasts, encourage them to tear apart the bread and enjoy every morsel of this warm deliciousness.

MAKES 6 TO 8 SERVINGS

1 round sourdough bread, at least 7 inches in diameter

2 tablespoons extra-virgin olive oil

¼ cup plus ¼ cup **fig jam**

1 8-ounce double- or triple-cream Brie cheese wheel

1 tablespoon chopped fresh chives

Heat the oven to 350°F. Line a sheet pan with aluminum foil.

Using a serrated knife, slice off ½ to ¾ inch from the top of the bread. Cut the top into wedges and set aside.

Center the Brie on top of the bread. Cut around the Brie to hollow out the bread so the cheese will fit snugly inside. Continue to hollow out the bread, taking care not to cut all the way through the bottom or the sides. Brush the inside of the bread with the oil. Spread ¼ cup fig jam on the bottom of the bread bowl. Carefully tear the hollowed-out bread into 1-inch pieces. Trim off and discard the top rind of the Brie wheel. Place the Brie, cut side up, inside the bread and transfer it to the prepared pan. Top the Brie with the remaining ¼ cup fig jam. Arrange the wedges and pieces of bread on the sheet pan to toast as the Brie melts.

Bake until the Brie is completely melted, 30 to 35 minutes, and the bread pieces are toasted. Sprinkle with chives before serving.

Party Cheese Ball

Cheese balls have long been a favorite party appetizer. Keep one on hand for last-minute gatherings or holiday festivities. In this recipe, cream cheese, two kinds of Cheddar, and large bacon pieces are blended and shaped into a ball. Just before serving, roll the ball in corn chips finely ground in a food processor for a nice crunch. Arrange on a platter surrounded by crackers, pretzels, and crudités. Pass glasses of Rosé Summer Spritzers (page 238).

MAKES 8 SERVINGS

½ pound bacon (about 8 slices), cut into 1-inch pieces

1 8-ounce package cream cheese, at room temperature

½ cup (2 ounces) shredded sharp Cheddar

½ cup **sharp Cheddar cheese spread**, at room temperature

¼ teaspoon freshly ground black pepper

½ cup finely ground corn chips

1 tablespoon chopped fresh flat-leaf parsley leaves

Cook the bacon in a skillet over medium heat until crisp, 12 to 15 minutes. Drain the bacon on a paper towel–lined plate and discard the fat.

Put the bacon, cream cheese, Cheddar, cheese spread, and pepper in a bowl. Using a spatula, mix until evenly incorporated. Line a small bowl with plastic wrap. Spoon the mixture into the plastic and close it tightly to shape the mixture into a ball. Refrigerate for 4 hours or freeze for 1½ hours, until the ball is firm.

Combine the crushed corn chips and parsley on a plate. Remove the plastic wrap, then roll the ball in the chip-parsley mixture to coat evenly all over, pressing firmly so the crumbs stick. To serve, arrange on a cutting board.

Butternut Squash Hummus

Since peeled and cubed butternut squash is now available year-round, you can serve this dip anytime. Sweet, nutty squash is roasted, then puréed with traditional hummus ingredients—chickpeas and tahini. A dusting of cayenne on the top gives the hummus a zippy kick and a pop of color. Surround the bowl with apple and pear slices, pita wedges, or colorful vegetable chips.

MAKES 3 CUPS

1 1-pound package **butternut squash** pieces (if large, cut into 1½-inch pieces)

1 tablespoon plus ¼ cup plus 2 tablespoons extra-virgin olive oil

½ teaspoon plus ¾ teaspoon kosher salt

¼ teaspoon plus ½ teaspoon freshly ground black pepper

1 15.5-ounce can **chickpeas**, rinsed and drained

3 garlic cloves

⅓ cup fresh lemon juice

¼ cup **tahini**

⅛ teaspoon cayenne

Heat the oven to 400°F. Line a sheet pan with aluminum foil.

Put the squash, 1 tablespoon oil, ½ teaspoon salt, and ¼ teaspoon pepper in a bowl and toss to coat. Arrange the squash in a single layer on the prepared pan. Bake until tender when pierced with a fork, 40 to 45 minutes. Set aside to cool.

Put the cooled squash, chickpeas, garlic, lemon juice, tahini, ¼ cup oil, ¼ cup water, and the remaining ¾ teaspoon salt and ½ teaspoon pepper into a food processor. Pulse until creamy or to the desired consistency.

Spoon the hummus into a serving dish, then drizzle on the remaining 2 tablespoons oil and sprinkle with the cayenne before serving. The hummus is best when just made, but it can be covered and refrigerated for 2 days and brought to room temperature before serving.

Nibble Board

For effortless entertaining, nibble boards are game changers. This bountiful board starts with rolled-and-sliced pinwheels of roast beef and American cheese. Then add hollowed-out and filled cherry tomatoes, all prepared ahead. Everything else is unwrapped or spooned from a jar and arranged on a big cutting board, platter, or even a sheet pan. Fill in the gaps with crackers, bowls of dips, breadsticks, olives, grapes . . . you name it. There are just two rules: The more, the better, and leave no space empty on your nibble board.

MAKES 6 TO 8 SERVINGS

⅓ cup **horseradish sauce**

8 slices roast beef

8 slices American cheese

12 cherry tomatoes

6 tablespoons **garlic-and-herbs spreadable cheese**

2 tablespoons crushed potato chips

8 ounces Gouda, cut into bite-size pieces

8 ounces sliced salami

1 cup roasted, salted shelled pistachios

1 cup dried apricots

Spread about 2 teaspoons of the horseradish sauce on a slice of roast beef. Top with 1 slice of American cheese. Roll into a log and then slice it into 5 pieces. Repeat with the remaining roast beef, horseradish sauce, and American cheese. Cover and refrigerate until needed.

Cut a thin slice off the tops of the cherry tomatoes. If necessary, cut off a thin slice on the bottom so the tomatoes sit without rolling. Using a small spoon, scoop out and discard the tomato pulp and seeds. Place the hollow tomatoes upside down on a paper towel to drain for 10 minutes. Spoon ½ tablespoon of the spreadable cheese into each tomato and sprinkle with some of the crushed potato chips. Cover and refrigerate until needed.

Arrange the Gouda, salami, pistachios, apricots, pinwheels, and stuffed tomatoes on a large platter or cutting board.

Buffalo Chicken Tachos

I do not want to live in a world without Tater Tots. Here's a new way to combine them with the classic flavors of Buffalo chicken wings. Use Tater Tots in place of tortilla chips and buffalo chicken sauce for taco sauce, and you have tachos. These ingredients, along with shredded rotisserie chicken, Cheddar, and diced celery, are layered and baked until hot. Top this gooey goodness with some blue cheese dressing and chopped scallions.

MAKES 10 SERVINGS

Vegetable oil spray

1 28-ounce package frozen **Tater Tots**

1 2½- to 3-pound **rotisserie chicken**, meat removed and shredded

⅔ cup **Buffalo wing sauce**

1½ cups (6 ounces) plus 1½ cups (6 ounces) shredded sharp Cheddar

1 cup **blue cheese crumbles**

1 cup **chopped celery**

⅔ cup **blue cheese dressing**

¼ cup thinly sliced scallions

Heat the oven to 425°F. Line a sheet pan with aluminum foil and coat it with vegetable oil spray.

Arrange the Tater Tots in a single layer on the prepared pan and bake until golden brown, 25 to 30 minutes.

While the Tater Tots are baking, combine the shredded chicken and the wing sauce in a bowl and toss well. Remove the sheet pan from the oven. Sprinkle 1½ cups Cheddar on the hot Tater Tots, followed by the chicken, then the remaining 1½ cups Cheddar, the crumbled blue cheese, and celery. Bake until the cheese is melted and the chicken is hot, about 15 minutes. Drizzle with the blue cheese dressing and scallions before spooning out servings.

D-I-Y Deviled Eggs

While the egg yolk filling with mayonnaise and mustard is classic and familiar, the imaginative toppings are anything but. Use these ideas or create your own do-it-yourself combinations. To save prep time, purchase bags of already hard-boiled and peeled eggs.

MAKES 24 SERVINGS

12 **hard-boiled and peeled eggs**, halved lengthwise

½ cup mayonnaise

2 teaspoons Dijon mustard

1 teaspoon apple cider vinegar

½ teaspoon freshly ground black pepper

2 or 3 radishes, shredded

3 bacon slices, cooked and crumbled

⅛ cup canned **crispy fried onions**

1 jalapeño, seeded and thinly sliced

2 teaspoons **capers**, rinsed

Gently remove the egg yolks from the whites. Put the yolks, mayonnaise, mustard, vinegar, and pepper in a bowl. Mash with a fork until smooth and creamy.

Using a pastry bag fitted with a tip, pipe about 1 tablespoon of the yolk mixture into each egg white half. (Alternatively, you can carefully spoon the filling into each half.) Garnish with the radishes, bacon, onions, jalapeño, and capers, or your choice of other creative toppings. Serve immediately. To prepare ahead, fill the whites with the yolk filling, cover, and refrigerate up to 24 hours. Add the toppings just before serving.

BREAKFAST:

RISE AND SHINE DELIGHTS

How do you start your day? A muffin and a cup of joe on the run? Griddle some pancakes? Cook up some grits and sausage? No matter what your morning routine is or what time it begins, refresh your morning meals with these new ideas.

While biscuit muffins made with a baking mix puff up in the oven, put together a quick sausage gravy to go with them. The Hawaiian Breakfast Bake with ham steak, canned pineapple, and packaged sweet rolls is ideal for a weekend breakfast. Elevate avocado toast by using bagels instead of sliced bread and topping each half with avocado spread, smoked salmon, and thinly sliced red onion. Season them with sprinkles of everything-but-the-bagel seasoning. Waffles with pumpkin purée and pumpkin pie spice can be enjoyed any season of the year. Granola ground in the food processor is combined with baking ingredients and frozen mixed berries to make the softest, most tender Granola-Berry Scones.

Supermarket shortcuts in these recipes save time and promise a super-satisfying breakfast.

Cheesy Grits Breakfast Bowls

Growing up down South, a bowl of grits mixed with some crispy, crumbled breakfast sausage and a side of buttered toast was a weekend favorite. These days, I stir in some grated cheese and top off the grits with a fried egg and some roasted red peppers for a colorful one-dish delight.

MAKES 4 SERVINGS

1 pound sage pork sausage

⅔ cup **quick-cooking grits**

¼ teaspoon plus ⅛ teaspoon freshly ground black pepper

1 cup (4 ounces) plus ½ cup (2 ounces) shredded extra-sharp white Cheddar

½ cup (4 ounces) cream cheese, at room temperature

1 tablespoon unsalted butter

4 large eggs

¼ cup chopped **roasted red peppers**

1 tablespoon chopped fresh chives

Put the sausage in a saucepan. Cook over medium heat, stirring occasionally to break up the pieces, until browned, about 10 minutes. Add 3¼ cups water, the grits, and ¼ teaspoon pepper to the saucepan and stir to combine. Bring to a boil, then reduce the heat to medium-low. Cook, stirring occasionally, until thick, about 5 minutes. Stir in 1 cup Cheddar and the cream cheese and continue to cook until the cheeses melt, about 3 minutes.

Melt the butter in a nonstick skillet over low heat. Crack the eggs into the skillet. Cover tightly with a lid and cook over low heat until the whites are set, about 2 minutes.

Divide the grits mixture among four bowls. Top each with a fried egg. Divide and sprinkle the remaining ½ cup Cheddar, the roasted red peppers, chives, and the remaining ⅛ teaspoon pepper over each serving.

Cheese, Please

In case you haven't noticed, I love cheese. While I'm all for convenience when it comes to cooking, I prefer to buy wedges, chunks, and bricks of Cheddar, Colby, Parmigiano-Reggiano, Monterey Jack, Asiago, and other hard cheeses and grate or shred them as needed, rather than using packaged shredded cheese. Potato starch and powdered cellulose are often added to packaged shredded cheeses as anticaking agents. These additives prevent cheeses from melting smoothly and evenly.

Soft, moist mozzarella is the one exception, because it can be difficult to shred, although you can grate mozzarella on the large holes of a box grater or in a food processor.

Grated Parmigiano-Reggiano and Asiago are exceptions to the measurements in the table below: 1 cup equals 3 ounces, not 4, but a bit more or less won't make a difference.

Because I do love cheese so much and use it frequently in these recipes, I'm including a handy chart to help you buy the right amounts.

WEIGHT	VOLUME
1 pound cheese	4 cups shredded
8 ounces	2 cups shredded
4 ounces	1 cup shredded
3 ounces	¾ cup shredded
2 ounces	½ cup shredded
1 ½ ounces	⅓ cup shredded
1 ounce	¼ cup shredded

Drop Biscuits with Cheese and Sausage Gravy

The dough for these time-saving drop biscuits is scooped and "dropped" onto a sheet pan, rather than rolled out and cut into circles. Make the savory gravy while the biscuits are baking. And I am serious about my gravy. To eat these the Southern way, split the biscuit through the center, ladle on the gravy, and enjoy with a knife and fork.

MAKES 5 OR 6 SERVINGS

Vegetable oil spray

2¼ cups **Bisquick** baking mix

1 cup (4 ounces) shredded extra-sharp Cheddar

1½ tablespoons plus 2 teaspoons **freeze-dried chives**

½ teaspoon kosher salt

¼ teaspoon freshly ground black pepper

⅔ cup milk

2 tablespoons plus 2 tablespoons unsalted butter, melted

8 ounces ground pork sausage

1 2.64-ounce packet **country gravy mix**

Heat the oven to 400°F. Line a sheet pan with parchment paper. Lightly grease the paper with vegetable oil spray.

Mix together the baking mix, cheese, 1½ tablespoons chives, salt, and pepper in a bowl. Stir in the milk and 2 tablespoons melted butter until fully incorporated. The dough will be very sticky. For each biscuit, drop 2 tablespoons of dough onto the prepared sheet pan, spacing them about 2 inches apart. Bake until light golden brown around the edges, 11 to 13 minutes. Remove from the oven. Brush with the remaining 2 tablespoons melted butter. Set aside.

Cook the sausage in a saucepan over medium-high heat, breaking it into small pieces and stirring occasionally, until browned, 6 to 8 minutes. Add the gravy packet contents to the saucepan and prepare according to the package instructions.

Split and arrange the biscuits on plates. Pour the gravy over the biscuits and sprinkle with the remaining 2 teaspoons chives.

Hawaiian Breakfast Bake

Say "aloha" with this morning bread pudding inspired by my trips to Hawaii. Every meal was enjoyed under swaying palm trees and turquoise skies, while the surf crashed on the shore. The subtle sweetness comes from using Hawaiian sweet rolls and pineapple chunks combined with some savory ham. Here's to paradise on a plate.

MAKES 8 SERVINGS

Vegetable oil spray

1 8-ounce can **pineapple chunks**, drained
and juice reserved

1⅛ cups confectioners' sugar

1¼ cups milk

1 cup heavy cream

5 large eggs

4 tablespoons (½ stick) unsalted butter, melted

½ teaspoon kosher salt

12 ounces **precooked ham steak**, cut into ½-inch pieces

20 **Original Hawaiian Sweet Rolls**, cut each into quarters

Heat the oven to 350°F. Coat a 9 × 13-inch baking dish with vegetable oil spray.

Whisk together 3 tablespoons of the reserved pineapple juice and the confectioners' sugar in a bowl. Set aside.

Whisk together the remaining pineapple juice, milk, cream, eggs, melted butter, and salt in a bowl. Add the pineapple chunks, ham, and roll pieces and gently toss to combine. Pour the mixture, evenly distributed, into the prepared dish.

Bake until golden brown and the center is set, 50 to 55 minutes. Remove from the oven and drizzle with the pineapple glaze before serving.

Oat-Banana Pancakes with Peanut Butter Syrup

You'll go bananas for breakfast with these hearty pancakes and a topping of peanut butter and pancake syrup. Gluten-free oat flour can be found in the baking aisle. When you add a side of bacon, you're channeling Elvis and a morning meal that The King would have loved. Feel free to double the recipe and make a tall stack.

MAKES 8 PANCAKES

8 bacon slices (about ½ pound)

½ cup pancake syrup

2 tablespoons creamy peanut butter

1 ripe whole banana plus 2 ripe bananas, cut into ¼-inch slices

2 large eggs

3 tablespoons milk

1 teaspoon pure vanilla extract

¾ cup oat flour

1 teaspoon baking powder

¾ teaspoon ground cinnamon

Cook the bacon in a skillet over medium heat until crisp, 12 to 15 minutes. Drain the bacon on a paper towel-lined plate and discard the fat.

While the bacon is cooking, whisk the syrup and peanut butter together in a bowl until smooth. Set aside.

Put the whole banana, eggs, milk, vanilla, oat flour, baking powder, and cinnamon in a blender. Blend on high speed until the batter is smooth, about 1 minute. Let the batter sit in the blender for 5 minutes.

Heat a large nonstick skillet over medium heat. When the pan is hot, pour in ¼ cup batter for each pancake. Cook for 45 seconds, until slightly puffed. Flip the pancakes and cook until golden brown and cooked through, about 45 seconds more.

Place the sliced bananas between and on top of 2 pancakes for each serving. Drizzle on the peanut butter syrup and serve with the bacon.

Pumpkin Waffles
with Spiced Honey Butter

As soon as the calendar turns to September, pumpkin and its companion spices like nutmeg and cinnamon can be found in everything from coffee blends to ice cream to donuts. A batter of canned pumpkin purée, pancake/waffle mix, and pumpkin pie spices gets these quickly from the waffle iron to the table. Yes, I'm giving you permission to have waffles for lunch or dinner.

MAKES 3 WAFFLES

6 tablespoons (¾ stick) unsalted butter, at room temperature

3 tablespoons honey, plus extra for drizzling

3 tablespoons plus ½ cup canned **pumpkin purée** (not pumpkin pie filling)

½ teaspoon plus 1½ teaspoons **pumpkin pie spice**

1⅔ cups **just-add-water pancake/waffle mix**

2 tablespoons (packed) light brown sugar

¾ teaspoon ground cinnamon

2½ tablespoons vegetable oil

1 teaspoon pure vanilla extract

3 tablespoons chopped pecans, toasted

Put the butter, honey, 3 tablespoons pumpkin purée, and ½ teaspoon pumpkin pie spice in a bowl and mix until creamy and combined. Set the honey butter aside.

Whisk together the pancake/waffle mix, brown sugar, cinnamon, and the remaining 1½ teaspoons pumpkin pie spice in a bowl. Stir in the oil, vanilla, ¾ cup water, and the remaining ½ cup pumpkin purée and mix until combined. Do not overmix.

Heat the waffle iron, greasing, if necessary, per the manufacturer's instructions. Pour the batter onto the waffle iron and cook according to the manufacturer's instructions. Spoon the spiced honey butter onto the hot waffles, sprinkle with pecans, and drizzle with additional honey before serving.

Tomato-Cheese Galette

A galette is a French free-form tart that requires no special pan and no crimping. While fillings can be sweet or savory, I'm partial to this tomato-and-cheese combination. Use the best, ripest heirloom tomatoes in any color—red, yellow, burgundy—that you can find at the grocery store or farmers' market. Draining the sliced tomatoes well prevents the crust from becoming soggy.

MAKES 4 TO 6 SERVINGS

1¼ pounds (about 3) heirloom tomatoes, cut into ¼-inch slices

1 tablespoon kosher salt

1 **refrigerated pie crust**, at room temperature

All-purpose flour, for rolling

1 5-ounce container **garlic-and-herbs spreadable cheese**, at room temperature

¾ cup (3 ounces) shredded Cheddar

¼ teaspoon freshly ground black pepper

1 large egg, lightly beaten

1 scallion, thinly sliced

Put the sliced tomatoes in a colander. Sprinkle with the salt and toss gently. Let the tomatoes sit for 15 minutes to drain some of their liquid. Arrange the tomatoes on paper towels to absorb more of the liquid and let sit for 15 minutes more.

Unroll the pie crust onto a piece of parchment paper. Lightly flour both sides of the dough. Using a rolling pin, roll the dough into a 12-inch round. Transfer the paper with the dough onto a large sheet pan.

Mix together the spreadable cheese, Cheddar, and pepper in a bowl. Using a spatula, spread the cheese mixture on the crust, leaving a 2-inch border. Arrange the tomatoes on top of the cheese mixture. Gently fold the border up and over the filling, pleating it as you go along. The center will be open. Using a pastry brush, brush the edges with the beaten egg. Refrigerate the galette for 15 minutes.

Position an oven rack in the lower third of the oven. Heat the oven to 400°F. Bake the galette until golden brown and cooked through, 50 to 55 minutes. Let cool on a wire rack. Garnish with the scallion before slicing and serving warm or at room temperature.

Granola-Berry Scones

These buttery scones have soft, tender centers and are golden brown on the outside. Finely grind some of your favorite granola in the food processor and combine it with the flour for more texture. Frozen mixed berries, rather than dried, help keep the scones moist.

MAKES 8 SCONES

Vegetable oil spray

1⅓ cups finely ground **granola**

1 cup all-purpose flour, plus more for rolling

⅓ cup sugar

1 tablespoon baking powder

1 teaspoon ground cinnamon

6 tablespoons (¾ stick) unsalted butter, cut into ½-inch cubes and frozen

⅓ cup plus 2 tablespoons heavy cream

1 tablespoon pure vanilla extract

⅔ cup **frozen mixed berries** (do not thaw)

Heat the oven to 375°F. Line a sheet pan with parchment paper and lightly coat it with vegetable oil spray.

Combine the ground granola, flour, sugar, baking powder, and cinnamon in the bowl of a food processor and pulse until mixed. Add the frozen butter cubes and pulse until the mixture is crumbly, 6 to 8 pulses. Pour the heavy cream and vanilla through the feed tube and pulse 10 to 12 times, just until the dough comes together but is still crumbly.

Turn the crumbly dough onto a lightly floured surface. Put the frozen berries on top and, using your hands, knead until the berries are incorporated and the dough comes together. Shape the dough into a 7-inch circle about 1 inch thick. Cut it into 8 wedges. Place the scones about 1 inch apart on the prepared sheet pan and bake until puffed and cooked through, 22 to 25 minutes. Cool completely on a wire rack before serving.

Avocado Bagel Toast

Layering some buttery, nutty, creamy avocado spread, thinly sliced smoked salmon, and everything-bagel topping on toasted bagels elevates this popular open-faced breakfast sandwich. Enjoy them Monday through Friday or share them at a weekend brunch.

MAKES 4 SERVINGS

2 ripe avocados, pitted and quartered

2 tablespoons fresh lemon juice

2 teaspoons plus 1 teaspoon **everything-but-the-bagel seasoning**

1½ teaspoons hot sauce

2 pumpernickel bagels, sliced in half crosswise

6 ounces thinly sliced smoked salmon

¼ cup **thinly sliced red onions**

1 radish, thinly sliced

2 teaspoons **capers**, rinsed

4 teaspoons fresh dill leaves

Put the avocado, lemon juice, 2 teaspoons bagel seasoning, and the hot sauce in a food processor and pulse until creamy.

Toast the bagel halves. Evenly spread each half with the avocado mixture. Divide and layer the salmon among the 4 bagel halves. Top each one with some of the red onion, radish, capers, dill, and the remaining 1 teaspoon bagel seasoning.

Chocolate-Peanut Butter Granola Bars

Most granola bars are dry, crumbly, and way too sugary for my taste. Chocolate chip, peanut butter, and coconut add just the right amount of sweetness to these moist, chewy bars. They keep well in an airtight container for nearly a week.

MAKES 8 BARS

Vegetable oil spray

2 cups old-fashioned oats

1 cup **sweetened shredded coconut**

2 large egg whites

½ cup (packed) light brown sugar

⅓ cup smooth or chunky peanut butter

¼ cup honey

1¼ teaspoons ground cinnamon

¼ teaspoon kosher salt

¾ cup milk chocolate chips, chilled (so they don't melt)

Heat the oven to 325°F. Lightly coat the bottom of a 9 × 9-inch baking pan with vegetable oil spray. Line the bottom and two sides of the baking pan with a piece of parchment paper. Lightly coat the paper with vegetable oil spray. Set aside.

Spread the oats and coconut on a sheet pan and bake until lightly browned, 11 to 12 minutes. Let cool for 3 minutes.

Whisk together the egg whites, brown sugar, peanut butter, honey, cinnamon, and salt in a bowl. Add the oat-coconut mixture and stir until the oats are coated. Stir in the chocolate chips until incorporated.

Evenly spread the batter into the prepared pan. Place a piece of plastic wrap over the top. Using your hands, firmly press down on the granola, packing it as tightly as possible. Remove and discard the plastic wrap. Bake until golden brown around the edges, 20 to 22 minutes. Remove the pan from the oven and let cool on a wire rack for 30 minutes. Turn the contents of the pan out onto a cutting board, remove the parchment paper, and flip the whole thing over. Slice into 8 bars. Cool completely before serving. Store in an airtight container up to 6 days at room temperature.

SOUPS:

SAVORY SPOONSFUL

While soups are often served as a first course, especially in restaurants, I often make a bowl of warming goodness my start-to-finish meal. What I love about these soups is not just how delicious they are but also how comforting and inviting they make my entire house smell while cooking.

Frozen vegetables, prepared sauce, and canned beans and tomatoes offer immediate gratification in Sloppy Joe Soup, a takeoff on the classic American sandwich. Pasta e Fagioli combines macaroni, canned tomatoes and beans, and broth for a no-fuss version of the Italian standard. Assemble cubes of leftover turkey and frozen vegetables for a hearty, satisfying chowder. Bright Carrot-Ginger Soup is nourishing to eat and warm and sunny to look at. Shrimp and Andouille Jambalaya starts with already diced vegetables and traditional Louisiana seasonings simmered with rice and shrimp.

Chopped herbs or scallions, a dusting of pepper or paprika, or a sprinkle of feta or Parmigiano-Reggiano makes any soup look restaurant worthy. Serve these with a wedge of Focaccia, toasted slices of rustic bread, or perhaps a square of cornbread.

Sloppy Joe Soup

Sloppy joe sandwiches were a weeknight favorite when I was growing up. While they're easy to make, they're not so easy to eat, because, well, they're sloppy and kind of soupy. So, I thought, why not turn a soupy sandwich into a satisfying soup? Using canned sloppy joe sauce, this soup is ready to ladle into bowls in less than forty-five minutes. FYI, this is a brothy soup rather than a thick chili, so it deserves some hearty bread or tender biscuits on the side.

MAKES 6 TO 8 SERVINGS

1 pound lean ground beef

2 cups **frozen chopped peppers and onions**

1 1.31-ounce packet **sloppy joe seasoning mix**

1 32-ounce box **low-sodium beef broth**

1 15.5-ounce can **kidney beans**, drained and rinsed

1 15-ounce can **sloppy joe sauce**

1 14.5-ounce can **petite diced tomatoes** with juices

1 teaspoon freshly ground black pepper

½ teaspoon kosher salt

3 tablespoons chopped fresh flat-leaf parsley leaves

In a large pot over medium-high heat, combine the beef, peppers and onions, and seasoning mix. Cook, stirring to break up the beef into smaller pieces, until the meat is cooked through and no longer pink, 5 to 6 minutes.

Stir in the broth, beans, sloppy joe sauce, tomatoes with their juices, pepper, and salt. Bring to a boil, reduce the heat to medium-low, and simmer for 20 minutes. Stir in the parsley. To serve, ladle into soup bowls.

Seafood Jambalaya

Like many Louisiana dishes, jambalaya starts with the "holy trinity" of diced onions, green peppers, and celery. Rice and seasonings go into the pot along with just about any meat, poultry, or seafood. Jambalaya gets its zip from the Creole seasoning and andouille sausage. Buttery garlic bread is perfect to serve on the side.

MAKES 6 TO 8 SERVINGS

1 tablespoon vegetable oil

1 13.5-ounce package andouille sausage, cut in ¼-inch rounds

2 cups **frozen chopped peppers and onions**

1 cup **chopped celery**

2 10.75-ounce cans **tomato soup**

2½ teaspoons **Creole seasoning**

1 pound (21/25 count) **frozen shrimp**, thawed, peeled and deveined

1 8.8-ounce package **Ben's Original Ready Rice**

¼ cup thinly sliced scallions

Heat the oil in a large pot over medium-high heat. Add the sausage and sauté until lightly browned, 4 to 5 minutes. Add the peppers and onions and celery and cook, stirring occasionally, for 5 minutes.

Stir in the tomato soup, 2½ cups water, and Creole seasoning. Bring to a boil, reduce the heat to medium-low, and simmer, stirring occasionally, until the vegetables are tender, 10 to 15 minutes.

Add the shrimp and rice and cook, stirring occasionally, until the shrimp are pink and cooked through, 5 minutes. Ladle into bowls and garnish with the scallions.

Creamy Chicken Pot Pie Soup with Dippers

As I wrote in Comfort Foods That Take You Home, *my mom always kept individual chicken pot pies in the freezer so we could have a hot meal when she worked late. Here's a spin on that childhood favorite—a quick, velvety soup with pieces of rotisserie chicken and plenty of frozen vegetables. Since there's no pastry "lid," make dippers from refrigerated pie crust to serve with this brothy soup.*

MAKES 4 TO 6 SERVINGS

1 **refrigerated pie crust**, at room temperature

1 large egg, beaten

¼ teaspoon plus ½ teaspoon freshly ground black pepper

2 teaspoons dried parsley flakes

2 tablepsoons vegetable oil

1 10-ounce package **mirepoix** (diced celery, onions, and carrots)

1 32-ounce box **low-sodium chicken broth**

2 cups shredded **rotisserie chicken** meat

1½ cups **frozen peas and carrots**

1 14.75-ounce can **cream of chicken soup**

Heat the oven to 400°F. Line a sheet pan with parchment paper.

Unroll the pie crust on a flat surface. Using a knife or pizza wheel, cut the dough into 16 equal-size triangles. Brush the triangles with the beaten egg. Evenly sprinkle the ¼ teaspoon black pepper and parsley flakes on top. Place the triangles on the prepared pan. Bake until golden brown, 8 to 10 minutes. Cool on a wire rack. These can be made ahead and stored in an airtight container for up to 2 days.

Heat the oil in a pot over medium-high heat. Add the mirepoix and cook until the onions are softened, about 5 minutes. Stir in the broth, chicken, peas and carrots, and the remaining ½ teaspoon pepper. Bring to a boil, reduce the heat to medium-low, and simmer until the vegetables are tender, about 15 minutes. Stir in the cream of chicken soup and cook until heated through, 2 to 3 minutes. Ladle into bowls and accompany with the dippers.

Turkey-Corn Chowder

Think of this thick, rich chowder like a blanket that's so warm and comforting after you've been outdoors on a cold winter day. By using supermarket shortcuts of already-carved turkey, chicken broth, and canned and frozen vegetables, this hearty dish is ready in just thirty minutes. Serve with a basket of crusty, rustic bread.

MAKES 8 SERVINGS

1 32-ounce box **low-sodium chicken broth**

2 8-ounce pouches **carved cooked turkey breast**, chopped

1 14.75-ounce can **Cream Style Sweet Corn**

1½ cups **frozen classic mixed vegetables**

1½ cups **frozen potatoes O'Brien with onions and peppers**

1 teaspoon dried thyme

¾ teaspoon kosher salt

½ teaspoon freshly ground black pepper

2½ tablespoons cornstarch

½ cup heavy cream

Put the broth, turkey, corn, mixed vegetables, potatoes, thyme, salt, and pepper in a large pot. Bring to a boil, then reduce the heat to medium-low. Simmer, stirring occasionally, 20 to 25 minutes.

Whisk together the cornstarch and ¼ cup water in a small bowl. Bring the chowder back to a boil over medium-high heat, then stir in the cornstarch slurry and cook for 1 minute. Reduce the heat to medium-low and stir in the cream for 1 minute. When thick and combined, serve hot.

Pasta e Fagioli

When translated, pasta e fagioli simply means "pasta and beans." This simple Italian soup delivers deeply satisfying flavors. Combine sautéed vegetables with broth, canned tomatoes, and white beans. The pasta—ditalini ("little thimbles") or small elbow macaroni—is cooked separately, then stirred into the soup just before serving. If desired, add a swirl of extra-virgin olive oil and some freshly grated Parmigiano-Reggiano to each bowl for a lovely finish. Pass a basket of homemade Focaccia (page 197).

MAKES 6 TO 8 SERVINGS

1½ teaspoons plus ½ teaspoon kosher salt

1 cup ditalini

1 tablespoon extra-virgin olive oil

1 10-ounce package **mirepoix** (diced celery, onion, carrot)

1 31-ounce can **refried beans**

5 cups **low-sodium chicken broth**

1 14.5-ounce can **petite diced tomatoes** with juices

1 teaspoon **Italian seasoning**

¾ teaspoon freshly ground black pepper

1 15.5-ounce can **small white beans**, drained and rinsed

Mirepoix

A number of savory recipes in *Half Homemade, Fully Delicious* start with sautéing a mixture of diced onion, carrots, and celery in olive oil (or another oil) to make a flavorful base for soups, stews, and other dishes. The French term for these small vegetable cubes is *mirepoix* (pronounced mihr-PWAH). Until recently, home cooks had to spend precious time peeling and chopping these vegetables. These days you'll find the ultimate supermarket shortcut—containers of these diced fresh vegetables—in your produce section.

Bring a large pot of water to a boil and add 1½ teaspoons salt. Add the ditalini and cook, stirring until tender, but still firm to the bite. Drain the ditalini in a colander, but do not rinse.

Heat the oil in the same pot over medium-high heat. Add the mirepoix and cook until the onions are softened, about 5 minutes.

Stir in the refried beans, broth, diced tomatoes with their juices, Italian seasoning, pepper, and the remaining ½ teaspoon salt. Bring to a boil, reduce the heat to medium-low, and simmer until the vegetables are tender, 25 to 30 minutes. Stir in the ditalini and white beans and cook until heated through, 4 to 5 minutes.

Broccoli, Cheddar, and Bacon Soup

Your friends and family members will think this rich and indulgent soup is made with heavy cream. It's not. When puréed, this soup becomes velvety smooth and silky. The bacon fat adds a gentle smoky flavor. Garnish the bowls with bits of bacon, some shredded Cheddar, and broccoli florets.

MAKES 4 SERVINGS

1 1-pound bag **frozen broccoli florets**

½ pound bacon (about 8 slices), cut into 1-inch pieces

½ cup **chopped yellow onions**

3 garlic cloves, minced

5 cups **low-sodium chicken broth**

¼ teaspoon kosher salt

¾ teaspoon freshly ground black pepper

1 cup (4 ounces) plus ½ cup (2 ounces) shredded sharp Cheddar

Set aside 2 broccoli florets to use as garnish. Once thawed, slice them in half vertically.

Cook the bacon in a large saucepan over medium heat until crisp, 12 to 15 minutes. Using a slotted spoon, remove the bacon to a paper towel–lined plate. Leave 2 tablespoons bacon fat in the saucepan and discard the rest.

Add the broccoli, onions, and garlic. Cook, stirring occasionally, until the onions are translucent, about 5 minutes. Add the broth, salt, and pepper. Bring to a boil, then reduce the heat to medium. Let the soup simmer until the broccoli is tender when pierced with a knife, 10 to 14 minutes.

Remove the saucepan from the heat. Add 1 cup shredded cheese. Use an immersion blender to purée the soup in the saucepan or, alternatively, pour the soup into a standing blender and blend until smooth. If using a blender, follow the manufacturer's instructions for blending hot liquids.

Ladle the soup into four bowls. Garnish with the bacon pieces, the remaining ½ cup shredded cheese, and the broccoli halves before serving.

Sweet Potato–Apple Soup

The burnt orange color and the sweet potato–apple flavors of autumn come together in this silky soup. Apples and apple juice add a bright flavor. (Use a sweet, firm apple, like McIntosh, rather a than too-tart Granny Smith or a too-soft Delicious variety.) Pass cups of this warming soup as a Halloween party starter. Or ladle the soup into your finest china bowls for Thanksgiving or any other dinner. Top each serving with some roasted pumpkin seeds.

MAKES 6 SERVINGS

4 tablespoons (½ stick) unsalted butter

1½ pounds peeled **sweet potatoes** chunks, cut into 1-inch pieces

1 McIntosh apple, peeled, cored and cut into 1-inch pieces

1 cup **chopped yellow onions**

1 teaspoon ground sage

1 32-ounce box **low-sodium vegetable broth**

2 cups apple juice

¾ teaspoon kosher salt

½ teaspoon freshly ground black pepper

¼ cup roasted pumpkin seeds

Melt the butter in a large pot over medium high heat. Add the sweet potatoes, apple, onions, and sage. Cook for 5 minutes, stirring occasionally. Add the broth, apple juice, salt, and pepper. Bring to a boil, then reduce the heat to medium-low and simmer until the sweet potatoes are tender when pierced with a fork, 30 to 35 minutes. Remove the pot from the heat and let cool for 15 minutes.

Purée the soup until smooth with an immersion blender or a standing blender, following the blender manufacturer's safety instructions for blending hot liquids. Ladle the soup into bowls and garnish with the pumpkin seeds before serving. The soup can be made ahead, refrigerated, and then gently reheated.

Carrot-Ginger Soup

Carrots have a unique earthy flavor, while ginger has zip. When the two are combined, their individual flavors not only stand out but also complement each other. The result is this colorful, tantalizing savory soup. A generous tablespoon of sour cream adds a mellow tang to each serving.

MAKES 4 TO 6 SERVINGS

1 tablespoon extra-virgin olive oil

1 pound **baby-cut carrots**

⅔ cup **chopped yellow onions**

2 garlic cloves, minced

1 tablespoon minced fresh ginger

5 cups **low-sodium vegetable broth**

¾ teaspoon kosher salt

¼ teaspoon freshly ground black pepper

1 tablespoon chopped fresh flat-leaf parsley leaves

4 to 6 tablespoons sour cream

Grating Fresh Ginger

You can buy grated or sliced ginger in a jar, but I prefer to prep my own when I want to add some zip to soups, stir-fries, and other dishes. Keep a knob of ginger wrapped in plastic in the freezer. Using a metal spoon, scrape the skin off as much of the ginger as you think you'll need, then grate the ginger on a Microplane zester.

Heat the oil in a large pot over medium heat. Add the carrots and cook for 5 minutes, stirring occasionally. Add the onions, garlic, and ginger and cook, stirring occasionally, for 5 minutes. Stir in the broth, salt, and pepper. Bring the soup to a boil, then reduce the heat to medium-low and simmer until the carrots are tender when pierced with a fork, 15 to 18 minutes. Remove the pot from the heat. Let cool for 15 minutes.

Purée the soup with an immersion blender or in a standing blender. (Follow the manufacturer's safety instructions when blending hot liquids.) Ladle the soup into bowls, garnish with the sour cream and parsley, and serve.

SALADS:

FRESH AND FABULOUS

Salad may not be the first thing that comes to mind when thinking about comfort food, but there are exceptions to every rule. And boy, are these salads satisfying.

Some summer days, I crave a Greek Salad with crisp bell peppers and cucumbers and salty olives and feta, as well as juicy tomatoes. Supermarket shortcuts of rotisserie chicken, canned beans, and barbecue ranch dressing make for a no-cook Barbecue Chicken Salad. Potato Salad with Bacon Dressing goes with any main dish. Anytime Autumn Salad includes the hearty, colorful vegetables we associate with fall, but we're fortunate that the ingredients are now available all year-round.

A big bowl of Creamy Fruit Salad made with fresh and canned fruit makes a great addition to your next buffet or potluck. They'll be licking the bowl when you're not looking.

Watermelon-Tomato Salad

Just reading the title of this refreshing salad reminds me of picnic tables laden with platters of D-I-Y Deviled Eggs (page 18), Cast-Iron Fried Chicken (page 161), and Creamy Corn off the Cob (page 179). Slices of sweet red watermelon and colorful heirloom tomatoes are combined here with crumbled salty goat cheese and a tangy dressing made with white balsamic vinegar. You can find peeled and sliced watermelon in the produce section, or purchase one-quarter of a melon and thinly slice. Summertime: The living just got tastier.

MAKES 6 SERVINGS

½ cup extra-virgin olive oil

¼ cup white balsamic vinegar

2 garlic cloves, peeled

½ teaspoon kosher salt

¼ teaspoon freshly ground black pepper

1½ pounds **seedless watermelon slices**

2 pounds (about 4 large) heirloom tomatoes, cut into ¼-inch slices

¼ cup **goat cheese crumbles**

2 tablespoons shelled and roasted sunflower seeds

1 tablespoon fresh chopped chives

Put the oil, vinegar, garlic, salt, and pepper in a blender. Blend until smooth, about 45 seconds. Set the dressing aside.

Alternate the watermelon and tomatoes slices on a platter. Drizzle on the dressing, then sprinkle with the goat cheese, sunflower seeds, and chives before serving.

Greek Salad

A few years ago, I took a cruise to some of the Greek islands. Every meal at quaint village restaurants started with a colorful salad of ripe vegetables dressed with olive oil and red wine vinegar. A block of feta was surrounded by the salad, and fragrant dried oregano was sprinkled on top. Using a fork, each person broke off a serving of cheese to eat with the salad. When cutting up the ripe tomatoes, be sure to add the juices to the bowl. So simple and so summery.

MAKES 6 TO 8 SERVINGS

3 tomatoes, cut into 1-inch pieces

1 cucumber, cut into 1-inch pieces

1 green bell pepper, cored, seeded, and cut into 1-inch pieces

½ cup **pitted kalamata olives**

⅓ cup **chopped red onions**

¼ cup extra-virgin olive oil

2 tablespoons red wine vinegar

¼ teaspoon kosher salt

1 8-ounce block feta

½ teaspoon dried oregano

Put the tomatoes, cucumber, green pepper, olives, and onions in a shallow serving bowl. Add the oil, vinegar, and salt and toss to coat. Place the block of feta in the center of the bowl, pushing aside the vegetables to make room. Sprinkle the oregano all over the vegetables and the cheese before serving.

Potato Salad with Bacon Dressing

If you're a "baconista" like me, there's no such thing as too much bacon. A meaty half pound of bacon slices here is tossed with warm potato cubes. The bacon drippings add a smoky flavor to the creamy, mustardy dressing. Serve this big, bold salad with Oven-Baked Baby Back Ribs (page 108), Cedar-Planked Grilled Salmon (page 119), or your favorite sandwich.

MAKES 6 SERVINGS

2 pounds red potatoes, cut into 1-inch pieces

1 tablespoon kosher salt

½ pound bacon (about 8 slices), cut into 1-inch pieces

½ cup sour cream

¼ cup apple cider vinegar

2 teaspoons Dijon mustard

1½ teaspoons ground ginger

½ teaspoon freshly ground black pepper

¼ cup chopped scallions

Put the potatoes and salt in a large pot. Add enough cold water to cover the potatoes by 1 inch. Bring to a boil, reduce the heat to medium, and simmer until potatoes can be easily pierced with a fork, about 15 minutes. Drain the potatoes and place them in a large bowl.

While the potatoes are cooking, cook the bacon pieces in a skillet over medium-high heat until crisp, 12 to 15 minutes. Using a slotted spoon, remove the bacon to a paper towel–lined plate. Pour the bacon fat from the skillet into a bowl.

Whisk together the bacon fat, sour cream, vinegar, mustard, ginger, and pepper until combined. Pour the dressing onto the potatoes and gently toss until evenly coated. Garnish with scallions and the cooked bacon before serving at room temperature.

Anytime Autumn Salad

It wasn't all that long ago that you could only buy butternut squash, kale, and even pears in the fall. Now, this sweet-and savory-stunner can be served year-round. Finish with a blue cheese dressing and a sprinkle of candied pecans. Serve with grilled steak or fish in the summer or accompanying the Herb-Roasted Turkey Breast (page 89) on a chilly evening.

MAKES 4 TO 6 SERVINGS

1 pound **peeled and cubed butternut squash**, cut into ½-inch pieces

1 tablespoon extra-virgin olive oil

½ teaspoon kosher salt

¼ teaspoon freshly ground black pepper

4 cups arugula

3 cups (1 medium) chopped radicchio

2 cups baby kale

⅔ cup **blue cheese dressing**

2 pears, quartered, cored, and cut into ½-inch pieces

¾ cup chopped **candied pecans**

Heat the oven to 400°F. Line a sheet pan with aluminum foil.

Put the butternut squash, oil, salt, and pepper in a bowl and toss to coat. Arrange the squash in a single layer on the prepared pan. Bake until the squash is tender when pierced with a fork, 25 to 30 minutes. Set the squash aside to cool.

Put the arugula, radicchio, baby kale, and blue cheese dressing in a bowl and toss until evenly coated.

Place the tossed greens into a salad bowl and top with the roasted squash. Garnish with pears and candied pecans before serving.

Tuna, White Beans, and Endive Salad

For a light meal, try this simple, eye-catching salad. Chunks of canned tuna, beans, and celery are layered on crisp endive leaves and peppery arugula. A lemony vinaigrette is spooned on top. Start the meal with bowls of warm Carrot-Ginger Soup (page 57) and squares of crusty Focaccia (page 197).

MAKES 4 TO 6 SERVINGS

¼ cup extra-virgin olive oil

¼ cup fresh lemon juice plus 1 tablespoon lemon zest

½ teaspoon kosher salt

¼ teaspoon freshly ground black pepper

2 cups arugula

2 Belgium endive (about 8 ounces), leaves separated

2 5-ounce cans **tuna, packed in water,** drained, and broken up into small pieces

⅔ cup canned **small white beans**, drained and rinsed

¼ cup **thinly sliced yellow or red onions**

½ cup **sliced celery**

Whisk the oil, lemon juice, zest, salt, and pepper together in a bowl. Set the dressing aside.

Place the arugula in the center of a platter. Arrange the endive leaves like flower petals around the arugula on the platter. Spoon the tuna pieces on top of the arugula and endive leaves. Spoon the beans, onions, and celery evenly over the salad. Pour the dressing on the salad before serving.

Steak Caesar Salad

Pile thinly sliced grilled skirt steak and grilled red onion slices on a bed of arugula or other sturdy greens for a main-course crowd-pleaser. The finishing touch is a Caesar dressing drizzled on top. While the grill is lit, if desired, brush some olive oil on slices of rustic bread and toast them to accompany this salad in place of the croutons.

MAKES 6 SERVINGS

1 2-pound skirt steak, halved crosswise

⅓ cup **Worcestershire sauce**

5 garlic cloves, minced

¾ teaspoon kosher salt

½ teaspoon freshly ground black pepper

3 heads romaine lettuce, chopped

1 cup **Caesar salad dressing**

2 cups **croutons**

½ cup **Parmigiano-Reggiano shavings**

Put the steak halves into a large resealable plastic bag. Add the Worcestershire sauce and garlic, seal the bag, and shake to coat. Put the bag in a baking dish (to catch any drips) and refrigerate for at least 2 hours or overnight.

Remove the steaks from the marinade and pat dry with paper towels. Discard the leftover marinade. Season the steaks with the salt and pepper.

Heat a skillet over medium-high heat. Add the steaks and cook 5 to 6 minutes per side for medium-rare, or to the desired doneness. Remove the steaks to a board and let rest for 5 minutes before slicing them thinly against the grain.

To assemble the salad, put the romaine lettuce and dressing into a bowl and toss to coat. Arrange the salad on a platter, then top with the sliced steak, croutons, and Parmigiano-Reggiano shavings. Serve immediately.

Barbecue Chicken Salad

For an updated chicken salad with Southwestern flavors and flair, combine black beans, corn kernels, and Cheddar with some rotisserie chicken. Toss it all with barbecue ranch dressing and spoon it onto a bed of romaine lettuce leaves. Potato sticks add some nice crunch. Get the party started with a platter of Tex-Mex Egg Rolls (page 2) and a pitcher of Orange Crush (page 241) cocktails.

MAKES 8 SERVINGS

1 2½- to 3-pound **rotisserie chicken**,
meat removed and shredded

½ cup plus ½ cup **barbecue sauce**

¼ cup plus ½ cup **ranch dressing**

1 8-ounce package **shredded iceberg lettuce**

1 cup (4 ounces) shredded extra-sharp Cheddar

½ cup canned **black beans**, drained and rinsed

½ cup canned **corn kernels**, drained

10 to 12 grape tomatoes, halved

1 ripe avocado, pitted, peeled, and chopped

1 cup **potato sticks**

Toss the shredded chicken with ½ cup barbecue sauce and ¼ cup ranch dressing in a large bowl. Set aside.

To assemble the salad, put the lettuce in a large bowl, then top with the chicken, cheese, black beans, and corn.

Whisk together the remaining ½ cup barbecue sauce and ½ cup ranch in a bowl and drizzle it over the salad, then top with the tomatoes and avocado. Garnish with potato sticks right before serving.

Creamy Fruit Salad

Crisp Granny Smith apples and canned pears and mandarin oranges are gently tossed with a whipped cream cheese dressing. While I love this combination, feel free to mix together your favorite fruits. Serve as a side dish or even dessert. Three tips for best results: Soak the apple pieces in lightly salted water to keep them crisp. Be sure to drain all the canned fruit well. Dry the cherries well so the white dressing doesn't turn pink.

MAKES 8 TO 10 SERVINGS

4 Granny Smith apples, peeled, cored, and cut into 1-inch pieces

1 teaspoon kosher salt

1 12-ounce tub cream cheese (original, not whipped), at room temperature

⅔ cup toasted chopped walnuts

1 15.25-ounce can **fruit cocktail in syrup**, well drained

1 15-ounce canned **pear halves in syrup**, cut into 1-inch pieces, well drained

1 10-ounce jar **maraschino cherries**, stemmed, well drained, and patted dry, divided

1 11-ounce can **mandarin orange segments**, well drained and divided

Put the apple pieces and salt in a bowl with just enough cold water to cover them. Let soak for 1 hour, then drain well in a colander.

Put the cream cheese in the bowl of an electric mixer. Beat on high until light and fluffy, about 2 minutes. Using a spatula, fold in the drained apples and walnuts. Gently fold in the fruit cocktail, pears, half of the maraschino cherries, and half of the orange segments. Spoon the mixture into your finest glass bowl. Garnish with the remaining cherries and oranges before serving.

CHICKEN & TURKEY:

FOR THE BIRDS

When I want a change from my tried-and-true poultry recipes, I look around for new tastes and reliable techniques. That's when I reach for some Marsala wine from Sicily, a package of presliced mushrooms, and a splash of cream to dress up boneless, skinless chicken thighs. For some Mediterranean flavors, fill colorful bell pepper halves with ground chicken, sun-dried tomato pesto, cooked rice, and feta crumbles before baking. A Moroccan spice blend adds unique layers of flavor to simmered chicken and vegetables.

Create a variety of textures by filling iceberg cups with savory ground chicken and crisp water chestnuts. Spatchcocking, or butterflying, chicken is a technique that allows the whole bird to better absorb the *mojo criollo*, a garlic-citrus marinade, and cook evenly, so all of the meat is moist and tender.

Turkey is a great blank canvas and takes well to all kinds of flavorings. Add barbecue seasoning to turkey burgers for some added punch. Onion soup mix and turkey gravy from a jar along with some frozen vegetables make a skillet of turkey meatballs a complete meal. Turn any dinner into a festive one with Herb-Roasted Turkey Breast.

When it comes to poultry, you won't have to wing it anymore.

Spatchcocked Fajita Chicken

To spatchcock means to split, but not separate, a bird down the back, and remove the backbone, so it lies flat. This technique allows the chicken to brown more evenly and cook faster. You can buy an already-spatchcocked chicken at the supermarket or do it yourself at home with kitchen shears. The bird is brined in mojo criollo, *a citrusy-garlicky marinade you can find in the international section, then roasted with fajita seasoning. Shred any leftovers and wrap in tortillas with all the fixings to make tacos.*

MAKES 6 SERVINGS

1 4- to 4½-pound spatchcocked or whole chicken

1 24.50-ounce bottle **mojo criollo marinade**

Vegetable oil spray

2 1-ounce packages **fajita seasoning mix**

3 tablespoons vegetable oil

2 red bell peppers, seeded and quartered

1 green bell pepper, seeded and quartered

1 yellow onion, quartered

To spatchcock the chicken, use kitchen shears and cut along each side of the backbone and remove it. With the breast facing up, press down firmly until you feel the breastbone crack. The chicken will now lie flat. Place the chicken in a large plastic bag and pour the mojo criollo over it. Seal the bag well, put it in a baking dish or bowl, and refrigerate overnight or for at least 8 hours.

Heat the oven to 400°F. Line a sheet pan with aluminum foil and coat it with vegetable oil spray. Remove the chicken from the marinade and discard. Pat the chicken dry with paper towels.

Whisk together the fajita seasoning and oil in a bowl. Brush the chicken all over with the fajita mixture. Place the chicken (breast side up), peppers, and onion on the prepared sheet pan. Roast until an instant-read thermometer inserted into the thickest part of the breast, but not touching the bone, registers 165°F, 50 to 55 minutes. Remove from the oven and let rest 5 minutes before slicing.

Chicken Tagine

"Tagine" refers to a Moroccan stew featuring poultry or meat with vegetables, olives, and ras el hanout, an easy-to-find spice blend of at least twelve aromatic seasonings. Tagine is also the name of the traditional cooking vessel the stew is prepared in, but all you need is a Dutch oven. Bone-in chicken thighs are simmered with the other ingredients. Serve each bowlful with a scoop of fluffy couscous or rice and a side of Green Beans, Red Onions, and Crisp Chickpeas (page 176).

MAKES 4 SERVINGS

2 pounds bone-in, skin-on chicken thighs, trimmed of any excess fat

1 teaspoon kosher salt

1 teaspoon freshly ground black pepper

1 cup thinly **sliced yellow onions**

1 cup **baby-cut carrots**

½ cup **low-sodium chicken broth**

½ cup **pitted green olives**

2 teaspoons **ras el hanout spice blend**

Juice and zest of 1 large lemon

1 tablespoon chopped fresh cilantro leaves

Season the chicken thighs with the salt and pepper. Heat a Dutch oven over medium heat. Add the chicken, skin side down, to the Dutch oven and cook until browned, about 5 minutes. Remove the chicken to a plate and set aside. Leave any drippings in the pot.

Add the onions and carrots to the same pot and cook, stirring occasionally, until the onions are translucent, 5 to 6 minutes. Stir in the broth, olives, spice mix, lemon juice, and zest.

Return the chicken to the pot, skin side up. Reduce the heat to medium-low, cover, and cook until the chicken is cooked through, about 35 minutes. Garnish with cilantro.

Chicken Marsala

Marsala, like sherry or port, is a fortified wine, which means that it has been blended with brandy or some other spirit. Dry Marsala has a nutty, brown-sugar flavor and is used in savory dishes like this classic. It's definitely worth buying a bottle of reasonably price Marsala, because—trust me—you'll want to make this every week. Accompany it with Smashed Potatoes with Pancetta and Gorgonzola (page 184) or serve atop some curly egg noodles.

MAKES 4 SERVINGS

4 4- to 6-ounce boneless, skinless chicken breasts

½ teaspoon plus ½ teaspoon plus ¼ teaspoon garlic salt

½ teaspoon plus ½ teaspoon plus ¼ teaspoon freshly ground black pepper

3 tablespoons all-purpose flour

2 tablespoons plus 1 tablespoon unsalted butter

1 8-ounce package **sliced white mushrooms**

¾ cup **low-sodium chicken broth**

½ cup dry Marsala

½ cup heavy cream

2 teaspoons fresh thyme leaves

Put 1 chicken breast on a piece of plastic wrap and cover with another piece of plastic wrap. Using a rolling pin, pound the chicken breast to a thickness of about ¼ inch. Repeat with the remaining chicken breasts. Remove the plastic wrap and season the chicken breasts with ½ teaspoon garlic salt and ½ teaspoon pepper.

Put the flour, ½ teaspoon garlic salt, and ½ teaspoon pepper in a shallow bowl and mix well. Dip each chicken breast into the flour, evenly coating both sides and shaking off any excess.

Melt 2 tablespoons butter in a large skillet over medium-high heat. Cook the chicken until golden brown, 2 to 2½ minutes per side. Put the chicken on a plate and set aside.

To the same skillet, add the mushrooms and cook, stirring occasionally, until they begin to soften, about 4 minutes. Stir in the broth, Marsala, cream, thyme, and the remaining 1 tablespoon butter, ¼ teaspoon garlic salt, and ¼ teaspoon pepper. Bring to a boil, lower the heat to medium-low, and simmer until the sauce has reduced by half, stirring occasionally, about 15 minutes. Return the chicken and any juices to the skillet and continue to cook until the chicken is cooked through, 2 to 3 minutes more. Spoon the sauce over the chicken before serving.

Chicken Lettuce Wraps

Ground chicken, diced canned water chestnuts, and seasonings are quickly sautéed, then spooned into crisp iceberg lettuce leaves. Let each person roll up their own, burrito-style. Feel free to add shredded carrots and purple cabbage for even more crunch. A word to the wise: Double the recipe—these disappear in no time.

MAKES 4 SERVINGS

1 tablespoon sesame oil

1 pound ground chicken

1 cup **chopped yellow onions**

1 tablespoon minced fresh ginger

1 8-ounce can **water chestnuts**, drained and chopped

⅓ cup **sweet chili sauce**

¼ cup **hoisin sauce**

3 tablespoons low-sodium soy sauce

1 head iceberg lettuce, leaves separated

Sesame seeds

Heat the oil in a skillet over medium-high heat. Add the chicken, onions, and ginger. Cook, stirring frequently to break up the chicken, until the meat is cooked through, 7 to 8 minutes.

Reduce the heat to medium. Stir in the water chestnuts, chili sauce, hoisin, and soy sauce. Cook, stirring occasionally, until the onions are tender, about 5 minutes.

To serve, spoon about 3 tablespoons of the chicken mixture into the center of each lettuce leaf, garnish with sesame seeds, and roll 'em up.

Peppers with Chicken, Rice, and Feta

Fill colorful red, yellow, and orange bell pepper halves with a mixture of ground chicken, cooked rice, and crumbled feta. The chicken makes for a much lighter dish than beef. No rice? Use leftover quinoa or couscous. The four peppers are cut in half to serve eight people. Start with the Watermelon-Tomato Salad (page 60).

MAKES 8 SERVINGS

1 tablespoon extra-virgin olive oil

8 ounces ground chicken

¾ cup **chopped red onions**

¼ teaspoon plus ¼ teaspoon kosher salt

½ teaspoon freshly ground black pepper

1 14.5-ounce can **diced tomatoes with basil, garlic, and oregano**

1 8.8-ounce package **Ben's Original Ready Rice**

1 6.7-ounce jar **sun-dried tomato pesto**

½ cup plus ⅓ cup **feta crumbles**

4 bell peppers, halved, cored, and seeded

Heat the oven to 375°F.

Heat the oil in a large skillet over medium-high heat. Add the chicken, onions, ¼ teaspoon salt, and the pepper and cook, stirring frequently, until the meat is cooked through, 4 to 5 minutes.

Remove the skillet from the heat and stir in the tomatoes and their juices, rice, pesto, ½ cup feta, and the remaining ¼ teaspoon salt. Divide the mixture evenly and spoon it into the 8 pepper halves. Arrange the peppers in a 9 × 13-inch baking dish. Add ½ cup water to the baking dish. Cover with aluminum foil. Bake until the peppers are tender when pierced with a fork, 45 to 50 minutes. Divide the remaining ⅓ cup feta crumbles among the pepper halves before serving.

Herb-Roasted Turkey Breast

When you want a dish for a small group or need some extra turkey for a crowd, this roast is perfect. Half of the herb–olive oil seasoning goes under the skin, while the rest is brushed on top of the breast. Pair with Sheet Pan Roasted Vegetables (page 175). Leftovers make great sandwiches.

MAKES 8 SERVINGS

1 6- to 7-pound whole bone-in turkey breast

⅓ cup extra-virgin olive oil

3 tablespoons minced fresh rosemary leaves

3 tablespoons chopped fresh sage leaves

4 garlic cloves, minced

2 0.7-ounce packages **Italian salad dressing & recipe mix**

1 teaspoon freshly ground black pepper

Heat the oven to 325°F. Dry the turkey breast with paper towels.

Whisk together the oil, rosemary, sage, garlic, salad dressing mix, and pepper in a bowl. With the top of the turkey breast facing you, gently slide your fingers between the skin and the meat, loosening the skin and creating a pocket. Put half of the herb mixture under the skin. Rub the remaining herb mixture all over the outside of the turkey breast.

Place the turkey, breast side up, in a roasting pan. Roast until an instant-read thermometer inserted into the thickest part of the breast, but not touching the bone, registers 165°F, 2 to 2¼ hours. Remove from the oven and let rest for 10 minutes before slicing.

Spice Up Your Cooking with Fresh Herbs

Fresh herbs add pizzazz, color, and flavor to all kinds of dishes. Scatter some chopped chives on dips and spreads for brightness. Use small amounts of woody herbs like rosemary when caramelizing onions or sautéing mushrooms. Toss grilled or roasted vegetables, pastas, and salads with chopped fresh flat-leaf parsley. Scatter thyme leaves on hearty soups, stews, and bean dishes. Sprinkle cilantro on Asian-, Mediterranean-, and Mexican-inspired dishes.

When buying bunches of basil or dill, look for perky ones with a fresh, clean fragrance. Once you get them home, loosely wrap each bunch in paper towels and place in an open plastic bag. Get in the habit of using them whenever you cook so they don't go to waste. Wash, stem, dry, and chop them just before using. Tie up herb stems with kitchen twine to flavor soups and stews.

Finally, start by adding a small amount; their flavors can vary depending on the variety and season. You can always add more.

Turkey Burgers

Turkey burgers were the first thing I prepared when In the Kitchen with David *debuted in 2009! While that recipe still can be found on QVC.com, it's time to revisit and reinvent this longtime favorite sandwich. Barbecue seasoning rub is combined with the ground turkey. I like to top my burger with some tangy barbecue sauce and crispy fried onions before serving it on a brioche bun.*

MAKES 4 SERVINGS

1 pound ground turkey

⅓ cup finely **chopped yellow onions**

2 tablespoons **dry barbecue rub**

½ teaspoon freshly ground black pepper

¼ teaspoon kosher salt

4 thick slices extra-sharp Cheddar

4 large lettuce leaves

4 brioche hamburger buns

¼ cup **barbecue sauce**

½ cup **crispy fried onions**

Using your hands, combine the turkey, onions, barbecue rub, pepper, and salt in a bowl. Do not overmix. Divide and shape the mixture into four ¾-inch-thick patties.

Heat a grill pan over medium heat. Add the burgers and cook until browned and cooked through, 4 to 5 minutes per side. During the last 45 seconds of cooking, top each burger with a slice of cheese.

To build the burgers, place a lettuce leaf on the bottom of each bun, then layer a cooked turkey burger, 1 tablespoon barbecue sauce, and 2 tablespoons fried onions on each. Finish the sandwich with the bun top and serve.

Skillet Turkey Meatballs with Potatoes and Onions

A package of onion soup mix perks up the flavor of these turkey meatballs. Once the meatballs are pan-seared, a handful of other supermarket shortcuts are added to the pan. This one-skillet dish makes for one fabulous family meal. Some Brazilian Cheese Bread (page 193) would be nice to sop up the gravy.

MAKES 6 SERVINGS

1 pound ground turkey

⅓ cup **plain bread crumbs**

¼ cup milk

1 large egg

1 1-ounce package **onion soup & dip mix**

½ teaspoon plus ½ teaspoon freshly ground black pepper

1 tablespoon vegetable oil

1 12-ounce jar **turkey gravy**

1 24-ounce package **frozen potato wedges**

1 cup **frozen pearl onions**

Put the turkey, bread crumbs, milk, egg, onion soup mix, and ½ teaspoon pepper in a bowl. Using clean hands, mix well to combine. Divide and shape the mixture into 12 meatballs.

Heat the oil in a large skillet over medium-high heat. Add the meatballs and cook, turning to brown on all sides, about 5 minutes.

Pour in the gravy and ½ cup water. Reduce the heat to medium-low. Add the potatoes, onions, and the remaining ½ teaspoon pepper. Cover and simmer until the meatballs are cooked through, 25 to 30 minutes, stirring once halfway through cooking. To serve, ladle into bowls.

BEEF & PORK:

TASTY CUTS

Nothing is more satisfying than savoring some tender short ribs, slicing into a juicy, pan-fried pork chop, or biting into falling-off-the-bone baby back ribs. I keep roasts, chops, ribs, and steaks in my freezer, because I never know what I'll be in the mood for or what I'll want to serve my guests.

Once you decide on a recipe, be sure to choose the right cut of meat for each particular technique. Skirt steak takes well to a quick sear. Combine cooked slices with vegetables and boiled ramen noodles for the fastest one-dish dinner ever. If you prefer low-and-slow oven cooking, try the baby back ribs. Or, let a pork butt with mustard and plenty of garlic simmer in a slow cooker. The stew gets a sweet-and-savory finish with Italian pickled vegetables and raisins. Season lean tenderloins with a rub and roast at a high temperature for just thirty minutes, then slice and serve with a tangy sauce.

Beef Ramen Bowls

Thank goodness for ramen noodles. At three for a dollar, these substantial, just-add-hot-water soup packages kept me fed on my meager salary at my first job out of college. These days, I jazz up the noodles with sliced steak, vegetables, and General Tso's sauce for a complete meal in a bowl.

MAKES 4 SERVINGS

3 3-ounce packages **ramen noodles**, seasoning packets discarded

1 tablespoon sesame oil

1¼ pounds skirt steak, trimmed of excess fat, cut first into 2-inch pieces and then into ¼-inch strips against the grain

¼ cup low-sodium soy sauce

¾ teaspoon freshly ground black pepper

2 cups thinly sliced mini mixed bell peppers

1 8-ounce package **sliced baby bella mushrooms**

1 medium red onion, thinly sliced

1 cup **General Tso's sauce**

¼ cup thinly sliced scallions

Bring a large pot of water to a boil. Add the noodles and cook, stirring until tender but still firm to the bite, 2½ to 3 minutes. Reserve ⅔ cup of the cooking water, then drain the noodles in a colander, but do not rinse.

Heat the sesame oil in the same pot over medium-high heat. Add the steak, soy sauce, and pepper. Cook, stirring frequently so all of the meat is coated, until the meat is medium-rare, 2 to 2½ minutes. Remove the steak to a plate.

Stir the peppers, mushrooms, and onion in the same pot. Reduce the heat to medium and cook until the onions are tender, 6 to 8 minutes. Add the General Tso's sauce, ⅔ cup reserved cooking water, noodles, and steak and cook, stirring frequently, until heated through, about 3 minutes. Divide among bowls, garnish with the scallions, and serve.

Pepper Steak

Chinese food is my go-to reward on Sunday evenings after my four-hour show, In the Kitchen with David. *Some days, I pick up takeout on the way home. Other times, I quickly throw together this easy-peasy stir-fry. I serve each portion with a scoop of rice and plenty of the savory sauce. For dessert, how about some Spice Cookies (page 212) and tea?*

MAKES 6 SERVINGS

¼ cup low-sodium soy sauce

2 teaspoons cornstarch

1 tablespoon vegetable oil

2 pounds flank steak, trimmed of excess fat and cut against the grain into 2 × ¼-inch pieces

1 1-ounce package **stir-fry seasoning mix**

1 teaspoon freshly ground black pepper

1 red bell pepper, seeded and thinly sliced

1 green bell pepper, seeded and thinly sliced

1 cup **thinly sliced yellow onions**

1 tablespoon minced fresh ginger

Whisk together the soy sauce, cornstarch, and 2 tablespoons water in a bowl. Set aside.

Heat the oil in a skillet over medium-high heat. Add the steak, seasoning mix, and pepper and cook, stirring regularly to break up the steak, until the meat is cooked through and no longer pink, 4 to 5 minutes. Remove the steak to a plate, leaving any juices in the pan. Add the peppers and onions. Cover the skillet, reduce the heat to medium, and cook, stirring occasionally, until tender, about 8 minutes. Add the steak, any juices on the plate, and the ginger and cook, stirring frequently, for 2 minutes. Pour in the soy sauce mixture and cook until the sauce has thickened, 1 to 2 minutes.

Pressure Cooker Beef Short Ribs

Hands down, braised short ribs are at the top of the list for my favorite cold-weather main course. I love how the meaty ribs easily partner with so many different flavor profiles, like smoky canned chipotle peppers. Serve these with Scalloped Potatoes with Smoked Gouda (page 183) so no gravy is left behind. Instead of oven-braising, which takes at least three hours, I use my pressure cooker and get the same results in a fraction of the time.

MAKES 4 SERVINGS

1 tablespoon vegetable oil

3½ to 4 pounds bone-in beef short ribs

1 teaspoon kosher salt

1 teaspoon freshly ground black pepper

1 cup **chopped yellow onions**

½ cup **low-sodium beef broth**

3 tablespoons tomato paste

6 garlic cloves, minced

2 canned **chipotle peppers in adobo**, chopped, plus 1 tablespoon adobo sauce

1 0.87-ounce package **brown gravy mix**

Heat the oil in a pressure cooker using the sauté setting. Season the short ribs with the salt and pepper. Add the short ribs to the pressure cooker and sear until browned on all sides, 10 to 15 minutes.

Put the onions, broth, tomato paste, garlic, chipotle peppers, and adobo sauce in the pressure cooker. Stir to incorporate. Close the lid, set to high pressure, and cook for 65 minutes. Do a natural release.

Remove the short ribs to a platter and cover with aluminum foil. Pour all of the liquid into a large measuring cup. Let it sit for 5 minutes and skim off any fat that rises to the surface. Pour 2 cups of the cooking liquid and the gravy mix into the pressure cooker. Select the sauté setting and bring the mixture to a boil. Whisk to combine and cook until thickened, about 5 minutes. Put the short ribs back into the pressure cooker to reheat, about 5 minutes. Serve the short ribs and gravy in bowls.

Slow Cooker Shredded Beef

When you're hankering for something hearty, bring out your slow cooker. This reliable appliance turns even the toughest cuts of meat into moist and tender goodness. Pile the shredded meat on sturdy sandwich rolls, use as an enchilada filling, or spoon onto cheesy grits. The four-hour wait is definitely worth it.

MAKES 6 TO 8 SERVINGS

1½ cups **chopped yellow onions**

1 cup **cola**

½ cup **steak sauce**

½ cup **chili sauce**

2 teaspoons smoked paprika

1 teaspoon kosher salt

1 teaspoon freshly ground black pepper

2½ to 3 pounds beef chuck, cut into 2-inch pieces

Whisk together the onions, cola, steak sauce, chili sauce, smoked paprika, salt, and pepper in a bowl. Put the beef into the slow cooker. Add the onion mixture. Cover and cook for 4 hours on high setting.

Using a slotted spoon, put the meat into a bowl and shred it using two forks. Return the beef to the slow cooker to reheat and mix with the gravy.

Oven-Baked Brisket

Guests will smell this amazing dish long before you open the front door to greet them. Start with a marinade of jerk seasoning and smoked paprika to add depth of flavor and just the right amount of warmth. Then braise the meat in a trio of tomato sauce, pineapple, and vinegar for some balanced sweet-and-sour goodness. Serve with wedges of Spinach Pie (page 180) or Anytime Autumn Salad (page 67). Be sure to set aside a few slices of brisket so you can enjoy a sandwich the next day.

MAKES 6 TO 8 SERVINGS

1 3½- to 4¼-pound beef brisket

½ cup **mild wet jerk seasoning**

1½ tablespoons smoked paprika

1 8-ounce can **tomato sauce**

1 8-ounce can **crushed pineapple**

½ cup **low-sodium beef broth**

2 tablespoons apple cider vinegar

Place the brisket in a shallow dish or container. Using your hands, rub the jerk seasoning and smoked paprika all over the brisket. Cover with plastic wrap and refrigerate at least 8 hours or overnight.

Heat the oven to 300°F.

Whisk together the tomato sauce, pineapple, broth, and vinegar in a 9 × 13-inch baking dish. Arrange the marinated brisket on top of the sauce. Cover tightly with aluminum foil and bake until the brisket is tender when pierced with a fork, 4½ to 5 hours.

Remove the brisket from the oven and let it rest, covered, at room temperature for 15 minutes. Thinly slice the brisket across the grain and serve with spoonsful of the sauce.

Sweet and Tangy Pork Tenderloins

Lean, quick-cooking pork tenderloins are ideal for weeknight meals, yet elegant enough for weekend dinner parties. Start with a dry rub that forms a crust to keep the pork's juices locked in. The sauce is a perfect balance of sweet preserves and tangy vinegar and mustard.

MAKES 6 SERVINGS

1 tablespoon plus 1 tablespoon vegetable oil

2 1-pound pork tenderloins, silver skin removed

3 tablespoons **McCormick Grill Mates Roasted Garlic & Herb Seasoning**

1 13-ounce jar **four fruit preserves**

⅔ cup **low-sodium chicken broth**

3 tablespoons apple cider vinegar

3 tablespoons unsalted butter

2 tablespoons Dijon mustard

¾ teaspoon minced fresh thyme leaves

¾ teaspoon freshly ground black pepper

Heat the oven to 425°F. Place a wire rack on an aluminum foil–lined sheet pan.

Heat 1 tablespoon oil in a skillet over high heat. Rub each tenderloin with ½ tablespoon oil, then sprinkle each with 1½ tablespoons seasoning. Sear the tenderloins on all sides until browned, about 5 minutes. Transfer the tenderloins to the wire rack on the prepared sheet pan. Bake until an instant-read thermometer inserted into the thickest part of the tenderloin registers 145°F, 20 to 25 minutes. Remove from the oven and let rest for 5 minutes before slicing.

While the pork is cooking, combine the preserves, broth, vinegar, butter, mustard, thyme, and pepper in a saucepan. Bring the mixture to a boil, then reduce the heat to medium. Cook, stirring occasionally, until the mixture has reduced and thickened slightly, 13 to 15 minutes. Serve with the sliced tenderloin.

Oven-Baked Baby Back Ribs with Lettuce Slaw

Racks of ribs are coated with Honeyracha Saucy Sauce, wrapped in foil, and then baked until the meat easily pulls away from the bones. When you read "sriracha," you might think, "Whoa, that's too much heat for me!" The Honeyracha adds just the right balance of heat and sweet. Serve with the iceberg lettuce slaw and plenty of extra napkins. If you're not getting sauce all over your face, you're doing it wrong.

MAKES 4 TO 6 SERVINGS

2 racks baby back pork ribs

2 teaspoons plus ½ teaspoon freshly ground black pepper

1 cup plus ½ cup **Honeyracha Saucy Sauce**

1 8-ounce package **shredded iceberg lettuce**

10 cherry tomatoes, halved

½ cup cooked and chopped bacon (about 4 slices)

½ cup **coleslaw dressing**

Heat the oven to 300°F.

To prepare the ribs, first remove the membrane covering the underside of the ribs: Push a butter knife under the membrane at the small end of the rack. Using a paper towel, grab the membrane and pull it off. Pat the ribs dry with a paper towel. Sprinkle each rack with 1 teaspoon pepper. Brush each rack on both sides with ½ cup of the sauce. Arrange each rack, bone side up, on large pieces of aluminum foil. Seal the foil packets completely. Place the foil packets on a sheet pan and bake until the meat is tender when pierced with a knife, 2¼ to 2½ hours.

Remove the ribs from the oven and unfold the foil. Heat the oven to broil. Turn the ribs meat side up, then brush the ribs with the remaining ½ cup sauce. Broil the uncovered ribs, 4 to 5 minutes, taking care that they don't burn. Let the ribs sit while preparing the salad.

Put the lettuce, tomatoes, bacon, coleslaw dressing, and the remaining ½ teaspoon pepper in a bowl. Mix to combine. Serve with the ribs.

Bourbon-Glazed Pork Chops

My mom's pork chops were simply seasoned with salt, pepper, and garlic powder, then panfried. Since they cooked in no time, she made them weekly to feed her three hungry kids. Now, when I panfry pork chops, I dress them up with some duck sauce, a splash of bourbon, and a good sprinkle of five-spice powder. And, Mom, don't worry, I always make a green vegetable—broccoli or asparagus—to round out the meal.

MAKES 4 SERVINGS

½ cup **duck sauce**

1 tablespoon bourbon

2 teaspoons low-sodium soy sauce

1½ teaspoons minced fresh ginger

¼ teaspoon **five-spice powder**

1 tablespoon vegetable oil

4 7- to 8-ounce boneless pork loin chops

1 teaspoon kosher salt

¾ teaspoon freshly ground black pepper

¼ cup thinly sliced scallions

Whisk together the duck sauce, bourbon, soy sauce, ginger, and five-spice powder in a bowl. Set the sauce mixture aside.

Heat the oil in a skillet over medium-high heat. Season the pork chops with the salt and pepper. Put the chops in the skillet and sear until browned on both sides, 2½ to 3 minutes per side.

Add the duck sauce mixture and reduce the heat to medium-low. Cover the skillet and cook for 8 to 10 minutes. Garnish with the scallions before serving.

Slow Cooker Pork Stew

South Carolina barbecue is distinguished by its vinegary, golden mustard sauce known as Carolina gold sauce. When those savory ingredients are combined with giardiniera (Italian pickled vegetables) and raisins, this comforting stew stands out for its unexpected burst of sweet-and-sour flavors.

Although you'll be tempted, don't lift the lid while this cooks, because you want to maintain an even temperature. Serve with rice or with mashed potatoes and some Cathead Biscuits (page 190).

MAKES 8 SERVINGS

½ cup yellow mustard

½ cup (packed) light brown sugar

8 garlic cloves, minced

1 tablespoon freshly ground black pepper

1 5-pound boneless pork butt, netting removed and trimmed of excess fat

1 32-ounce jar **Italian mix giardiniera**, drained

1 cup **chopped yellow onions**

½ cup raisins

2 **chicken-flavor bouillon cubes**

Whisk together the mustard, brown sugar, garlic, and pepper in a bowl.

Place the pork in the slow cooker. Spread the mustard mixture on the pork. Cover and cook on high setting for 2½ hours. Stir the giardiniera, onions, raisins, and bouillon cubes into the slow cooker. Cover and cook for an additional 3½ hours, or until the pork is fork-tender and easily pulls apart. Using tongs, break the pork into small pieces before serving.

SEAFOOD:

OCEANS OF FLAVOR

Most fish and shellfish dishes are simple and ready in less than thirty minutes. Lemon-Pepper Roast Cod is cooked in twelve to fifteen minutes. If you have some frozen scallops or shrimp on hand, Pan-Seared Scallops with Bacon and Citrus Butter as well as Southwestern Skillet Scampi both come together quickly for weeknight meals.

For fancier meals that make a statement, seafood takes well to getting dressed up for special occasions. Salmon remains tender and moist under a blanket of shredded potatoes. Crabmeat elevates creamy mac 'n' cheese into an elegant dish you can proudly serve at a dinner party. Celebrate the flavors of the seas with a creamy mix of shrimp, clams, and lobster tossed with linguine.

Potato-Crusted Salmon Fillets

A crusty topping of shredded hash browns turns ho-hum salmon fillets into an elegant dish. The potatoes become crispy, while keeping the salmon moist and tender. Serve with Sheet Pan Roasted Vegetables (page 175) or a garden salad.

MAKES 4 SERVINGS

---

1 cup **frozen shredded hash brown potatoes**, thawed

⅓ cup mayonnaise

2 tablespoons **horseradish**, well drained

1 teaspoon freshly ground black pepper

1 teaspoon onion powder

¾ teaspoon kosher salt

4 6- to 7-ounce salmon fillets, skin removed

1 tablespoon vegetable oil

2 teaspoons chopped fresh dill

Mix together the hash brown potatoes, mayonnaise, horseradish, pepper, onion powder, and salt in a bowl. Divide and spread the potato mixture on the top side of each salmon fillet. Heat the oil in a large skillet over medium heat. Using a spatula, gently put the salmon, potato side down, in the skillet and sear until golden brown and a crust forms, 4 to 5 minutes. Turn the salmon fillets carefully and cook for an additional 4 to 5 minutes. Garnish with fresh dill before serving.

Cedar-Planked Grilled Salmon

Grilling food on thin cedar planks delivers a slightly smoky flavor to fish, meat, and even vegetables. This technique allows for low-and-slow cooking, and your food won't stick to the grill. A salmon fillet with a honey-mustard glaze served on a lightly charred wood plank makes a stunning presentation.

MAKES 2 SERVINGS

2 11-inch untreated cedar grilling planks

2 6- to 7-ounce salmon fillets, skin removed

½ teaspoon kosher salt

½ teaspoon freshly ground black pepper

1 8-ounce can **pineapple slices,** drained

3 tablespoons **honey mustard**

6 sprigs fresh thyme

4 lemon slices

1 red bell pepper, seeded and quartered

Wood Plank Grilling

Choose untreated planks that are at least ½ inch larger than the piece of food you're grilling. They're sold in hardware stores and many supermarkets.

Pick a type of wood that goes well with the food. Traditional cedar gives salmon a gentle smokiness, cherry goes well with poultry, or pair beef with hickory.

Immerse the planks in water and soak for at least 1 hour before using to keep them from catching fire and the food from burning.

Submerge the planks in water and soak for at least 1 hour.

Heat the grill to medium-high heat, 350°F to 400°F. Put the planks on the grill and heat for 2 minutes on each side.

Season the salmon with the salt and pepper. On each plank, arrange 2 pineapple slices side by side with a salmon fillet on top. Spread 1½ tablespoons honey mustard on each fillet. Top each with 3 sprigs thyme and 2 lemon slices. Arrange the red pepper quarters next to the fillets.

Put the planks on the grill and close the lid. After 20 minutes, insert an instant-read thermometer until the thickest part of the salmon registers 145°F.

Lemon-Pepper Roast Cod

Lean and meaty, cod is readily available year-round. This versatile fish can be poached, broiled, fried, or, as here, roasted with a lemony, peppery compound butter. Haddock, striped bass, or mahi mahi makes a good stand-in for this super-quick main course. How long the fish is cooked depends on the fillet's thickness. Start by roasting for less time; you can always put the cod back in the oven for a few more minutes. Start with the showstopping Anytime Autumn Salad (page 67).

MAKES 4 SERVINGS

4 tablespoons (½ stick) unsalted butter, at room temperature

¼ cup chopped fresh basil leaves

2 tablespoons lemon zest

2 garlic cloves, minced

1 teaspoon kosher salt

1 teaspoon freshly ground black pepper

½ teaspoon paprika

4 6- to 7-ounce cod fillets

1 lemon, quartered

Heat the oven to 400°F.

Put the butter, basil, lemon zest, garlic, salt, pepper, and paprika in a bowl to make a compound butter. Mash with a fork to combine. Set the butter aside.

Arrange the fillets in a single layer in a baking dish. Spread the compound butter on top of the fillets. Bake until the cod is cooked through and easily flakes with a fork, 12 to 15 minutes, depending on the thickness of the fillets. Garnish with lemon quarters.

Panfried Catfish with Tartar Sauce

On special occasions when Mom took us out to eat, we usually went to a fish camp. These casual, family-friendly seafood restaurants are still popular throughout North Carolina. We always ordered the golden fried catfish, served in an oval, red-plastic basket lined with red-and-white checkered paper. To re-create those memories, I dredge and quickly panfry catfish fillets and serve them with homemade tartar sauce, hush puppies, and coleslaw. I like tangy homemade tartar sauce, but feel free to buy it.

MAKES 4 SERVINGS

⅓ cup mayonnaise

⅓ cup **dill pickle relish**

Juice and zest of 1 large lemon

2 teaspoons Dijon mustard

¼ teaspoon onion powder

¼ teaspoon freshly ground black pepper

⅔ cup **New Orleans Style Fish Fry Seafood Breading Mix**

4 6- to 7-ounce catfish fillets

¼ cup vegetable oil

Whisk together the mayonnaise, relish, lemon juice, lemon zest, mustard, onion powder, and pepper in a bowl until well combined. Set the tartar sauce aside.

Put the breading mix in a shallow bowl. Dip each catfish fillet into the breading mix, evenly coating both sides and shaking off any excess.

Heat ¼ inch vegetable oil in a large skillet over medium heat. Add the catfish fillets to the skillet and cook until golden brown, carefully turning once, 3 to 4 minutes per side. Drain briefly on paper towels. Serve with the tartar sauce.

Crab Mac 'n' Cheese

People who take mac 'n' cheese as seriously as I do sometimes add another spin to it, like crabmeat. Every tube of ziti in this luxurious dish bursts with some creamy pimiento cheese, Alfredo sauce, and bits of delicate crabmeat.

MAKES 8 TO 10 SERVINGS

1 tablespoon kosher salt

1 pound ziti

1 15-ounce jar **Alfredo sauce**

1 12-ounce container **pimiento cheese spread**

1 12-ounce can evaporated milk

1 cup **frozen diced fire-roasted red bell peppers**

1 tablespoon plus 1 teaspoon **Cajun seasoning**

1 16-ounce container lump crabmeat, picked over to remove any shells

2 tablespoons chopped fresh chives

Bring a large pot of water to a boil. Add the salt and ziti and cook, stirring occasionally, until tender but still firm to the bite. Remove ½ cup of the pasta cooking water and set aside. Drain the ziti in a colander, but do not rinse.

Put the Alfredo sauce, pimiento cheese spread, evaporated milk, red peppers, ½ cup reserved pasta cooking water, and the Cajun seasoning in the same large pot over medium heat. Cook, stirring frequently, until the sauce is creamy and well blended, 5 to 6 minutes. Add the ziti and crabmeat to the pot and simmer until heated through, stirring occasionally. Sprinkle with chives for garnish.

Southwestern Skillet Scampi

Instead of the traditional garlic butter–white wine combo, this shrimp dish takes a detour to the Southwest with salsa, black beans, and green chiles. Take care not to overcook the shrimp. They're done as soon as they turn opaque white and slightly pink. This dish is colorful and oh-so-flavorful.

MAKES 6 SERVINGS

1 tablespoon vegetable oil

2 pounds (21/25 count) **frozen shrimp**, thawed, peeled, and deveined

1 teaspoon kosher salt

1 teaspoon freshly ground black pepper

1 16-ounce container **fresh tomato salsa**

1 15-ounce can **black beans**, drained and rinsed

1 4-ounce can **diced green chiles**

3 garlic cloves, minced

2 tablespoons chopped fresh cilantro leaves

1 tablespoon fresh lime juice

Heat the oil in a large skillet over medium-high heat. Add the shrimp, salt, and pepper. Cook, stirring frequently, until the shrimp are opaque and cooked through, about 4 minutes. Remove the shrimp to a plate.

Add the salsa, black beans, green chiles, and garlic to the skillet. Cook, stirring frequently, until heated through, 3 to 4 minutes. Return the shrimp and add the cilantro and lime juice to the skillet. Stir and heat just until warmed through.

Pan-Seared Scallops with Bacon and Citrus Butter

This recipe uses the larger and more available sea scallops, rather than small bay scallops. Fry some bacon, then sauté the scallops in the rendered fat for a smoky flavor. A pan sauce quickly comes together with some butter, orange juice, and a pinch of red pepper flakes. Serve on top of some orzo or rice for a quick yet elegant main course.

MAKES 6 SERVINGS

4 bacon slices, chopped

1½ pounds sea scallops, dried with paper towels

¾ teaspoon kosher salt

¾ teaspoon freshly ground black pepper

3 tablespoons unsalted butter

⅓ cup fresh orange juice

2 garlic cloves, minced

1 tablespoon chopped fresh tarragon leaves

Pinch of red pepper flakes

Cook the chopped bacon in a skillet over medium heat until crisp, 12 to 15 minutes. Using a slotted spoon, remove the bacon to a paper-towel lined plate. Leave 1 tablespoon bacon fat in the skillet and discard the rest.

Season the scallops with the salt and black pepper. Reheat the bacon fat in the same skillet over medium-high heat. Add the scallops in a single layer, leaving space between them. Cook just until golden brown on the outside and translucent in the center, about 2 minutes per side. Remove the scallops to a plate.

Reduce the heat to low. Add the butter, orange juice, garlic, tarragon, and red pepper flakes and whisk until the butter melts. Return the scallops to the skillet along with any juices on the plate and toss to combine. Divide the scallops and the sauce among six plates. Sprinkle with the bacon pieces before serving.

Linguine with Seafood

This creamy dish is so rich and luxurious, it's the pasta to serve when celebrating a birthday, anniversary, or other significant event. The prep time is reduced by using shelled and deveined shrimp, canned clams, and cooked lobster meat, all available at your local supermarket's seafood counter. Many markets will steam and crack the lobster, so all you have to do is remove the meat at home.

MAKES 6 SERVINGS

1 tablespoon kosher salt

1 pound linguine

1 10.5-ounce can **cream of shrimp soup**

5 garlic cloves, thinly sliced

1¼ teaspoons **Old Bay Seasoning**

1 10-ounce can **whole baby clams**, drained and liquid reserved

1 pound (31/35 count) **frozen shrimp**, thawed, peeled, and deveined

1 1-pound **cooked lobster**, meat removed and chopped

Juice and zest of 1 large lemon

2 tablespoons chopped fresh flat-leaf parsley leaves

Bring a large pot of water to a boil and add the salt. Add the linguine and cook, stirring occasionally until tender, but still firm to the bite. Reserve ½ cup of the cooking water, then drain the linguine in a colander, but do not rinse. Use the same pot to cook the seafood.

Put the soup, ½ cup reserved cooking water, the garlic, Old Bay, and reserved clam liquid in the same pot over medium-high heat. Bring to a boil, then reduce the heat to medium. Add the shrimp and clams to the pot and cook just until the shrimp are opaque, stirring frequently, 4 to 5 minutes. Stir in the linguine, lobster, lemon juice, lemon zest, and parsley and heat through. Make sure each serving includes some clams, shrimp, and lobster.

CASSEROLES:

GOT YOU COVERED

My mom always had some casseroles in the freezer to keep us well-fed during the busy week. Coming home to one of those favorite dishes reheating in the oven was like receiving a warm hug when I walked in the door. These convenient, low-maintenance casseroles are ideal for weeknight family meals, potluck gatherings, and holiday get-togethers. Most can be assembled ahead, refrigerated (or frozen), and reheated. Leftovers can be divvied up into smaller portions and sent home with those around your table. Here are some tips for successful results.

Use an ovenproof dish made of tempered glass, stoneware, cast-iron, or enameled cast-iron for even baking. While metal pans conduct heat well, they don't retain heat, and you want your casserole to stay hot through second servings.

Choose the right size baking dish. If you have a rectangle rather than oval dish, of course, you can use it. Or divide the mixture between two smaller dishes. Fill the pan no more than three-quarters of its height to keep the contents from overflowing in the oven.

Once the casserole comes out of the oven, allow it to sit at room temperature for about ten minutes before serving. Don't worry about the casserole losing heat; it won't cool down much in such a short amount of time. The bubbling sauce on top needs to be reabsorbed, and the entire dish needs to firm up so you can spoon out servings that hold their shape.

Ground Beef–Noodle Casserole

Generations of Midwestern cooks continue to hand down their versions of this hearty dish. One thing that all those recipes have in common is that they start with rich egg noodles, instead of pasta, and include ground beef. This version has a double dose of tomatoey flavor from canned soup and diced tomatoes and plenty of cheesy goodness. Serve with a crisp green salad.

MAKES 8 SERVINGS

1 tablespoon plus 1 teaspoon kosher salt

1 12-ounce package wide egg noodles

1 pound lean ground beef

2 cups **chopped yellow onions**

1 teaspoon plus ¾ teaspoon freshly ground black pepper

2 10.75-ounce cans **tomato soup**

1 14.5-ounce can **petite diced tomatoes**

1 cup (4 ounces) plus 1 cup (4 ounces) shredded extra sharp Cheddar

1 cup sour cream

2 tablespoons chopped fresh flat-leaf parsley leaves

Heat the oven to 375°F.

Bring a large pot of water to a boil and add 1 tablespoon salt. Add the egg noodles and cook, stirring occasionally, until the noodles are tender but still firm to the bite, 6 to 8 minutes. Before draining, remove 1⅓ cups of the pasta cooking water and set it aside. Drain the egg noodles in a colander, but do not rinse.

In the same pot over medium-high heat, put the beef, onions, 1 teaspoon pepper, and the remaining 1 teaspoon salt. Cook, stirring frequently to break up the beef into smaller pieces, until the meat is cooked through and no longer pink, 7 to 9 minutes. Turn off the heat.

Add the tomato soup, tomatoes with their juices, the 1⅓ cups reserved pasta cooking water, 1 cup Cheddar, the sour cream, the remaining ¾ teaspoon pepper, and the cooked noodles. Stir well to combine. Pour the mixture into a 9×13-inch baking dish. Cover with aluminum foil and bake for 30 minutes. Remove the foil and sprinkle the remaining 1 cup Cheddar evenly on top. Bake until heated through and the cheese is melted, about 5 minutes. Sprinkle with the parsley and let sit for 5 minutes before serving.

Beef Enchilada Bake

Ground beef, beans, enchilada sauce, and Cheddar are layered lasagna-style between corn tortillas in this Southwestern-inspired casserole. Once baked, be sure to add the toppings; they provide even more tastes and textures. Look for Mexican Cotija where other cheeses are sold. This dish can replace tacos on Tuesday. Or any other day of the week.

MAKES 8 TO 10 SERVINGS

1 pound lean ground beef

2 cups **chopped yellow onions**

2 19-ounce cans **red enchilada sauce**, divided into ¾ cup plus 4 cups

18 6-inch corn tortillas

1 15-ounce can **pinto beans**, rinsed and drained

2 4-ounce cans **diced green chiles**, drained

4 cups (1 pound) shredded sharp Cheddar, divided

1 2.25-ounce can **sliced black olives**, drained

¼ cup (¾ ounce) grated Cotija cheese

2 tablespoons chopped fresh cilantro leaves

Heat the oven to 350°F.

Heat a skillet over medium-high heat. Add the beef and onions and cook, stirring frequently to break up the meat, until the meat is no longer pink, 7 to 8 minutes. Drain any excess fat or liquid from the skillet. Stir in ¾ cup enchilada sauce.

Pour 1⅓ cups enchilada sauce into a 9 × 13-inch baking dish, spreading it evenly. Arrange 6 tortillas, slightly overlapping, to cover the bottom of the baking dish. Evenly spoon half of the beef mixture on top, followed by half of the beans, half of the chiles, and 1⅓ cups Cheddar. Arrange 6 tortillas on top, followed by 1 cup enchilada sauce, the remaining beef, beans, and chiles, and 1⅓ cups Cheddar. For the last layer, top with the remaining 6 tortillas and sauce.

Cover with aluminum foil and bake for 50 minutes. Remove the foil and sprinkle the remaining 1⅓ cups Cheddar on top. Bake until heated through and the Cheddar is melted, 10 to 15 minutes. Let the casserole sit for 10 minutes, then top with the black olives, Cotija, and cilantro before serving.

Full of Beans

Butternut Squash Hummus. Pasta e Fagioli. Sloppy Joe Soup. Beef Enchilada Bake. All of these recipes and many others take advantage of the ultimate supermarket shortcut—canned beans. Kidney, black, pinto, and small white (navy) beans, along with chickpeas, are inexpensive and keep a long time on your pantry shelf. No cooking is required; just open a can and drain and rinse before using. Beans can be mashed, puréed, or used whole. Versatile beans add flavor and texture to dips, salads, soups, stews, rice, and many other dishes.

Pour the contents of a can into a strainer and rinse the beans under cold water. Doing so removes excess sodium from the beans and refreshes them as well.

Any leftover beans can be stored in an airtight container and refrigerated for about a week.

Chili Cheese Dog Casserole

Dee. Lish. Us. That sums up what I love about this casserole. Hot dogs are individually wrapped in crescent roll dough and baked, then nestled into some warm canned chili and heated through. Before serving, top with pickles, corn chips, and scallions. If you're looking for a family-friendly dish that everyone can help with, you just found it.

MAKES 8 SERVINGS

2 15-ounce cans **mild chili**

1 8-ounce can refrigerated **Pillsbury Original Crescents**

8 bun-length hot dogs

1½ cups (6 ounces) shredded extra sharp Cheddar

⅓ cup **chopped red onions**

½ cup chopped **dill pickles**

½ cup crushed corn chips

2 tablespoons thinly sliced scallions

Heat the oven to 375°F. Line a sheet pan with aluminum foil.

Pour the chili into a 9 × 13-inch baking dish. Put the dish of chili in the oven to heat while preparing the wrapped hot dogs.

Separate the crescent rolls into 8 triangles. Wrap a triangle around each hot dog and press to seal. Place the wrapped hot dogs on the prepared sheet pan. Bake until the wrapped hot dogs are golden brown, 18 to 20 minutes.

Remove the dish with the chili from the oven. Sprinkle the cheese and red onions over the chili. Arrange the hot dogs on top in a single layer. Bake until the cheese is melted, 3 to 5 minutes. Garnish with the pickles, corn chips, and scallions before spooning out servings.

Chicken-Vermicelli Casserole

Sean Hagan, producer of In the Kitchen with David, *brought his family's favorite casserole to a gathering when a bunch of my QVC pals got together for a "Friendsgiving" potluck dinner. Shredded meat from a rotisserie chicken is combined with vermicelli, chicken broth, onions, and sharp white Cheddar and then baked. If you can't find vermicelli, use any thinner-than-spaghetti pasta, like angel hair. If you'd like a bit more richness, sprinkle one-half cup grated Parmigiano-Reggiano on top once the casserole comes out of the oven. Trust me, no calorie is left behind with this one.*

MAKES 8 SERVINGS

1 tablespoon plus 1 teaspoon kosher salt

8 ounces (½ box) vermicelli, broken in half

6 tablespoons (¾ stick) unsalted butter

1 cup **chopped yellow onions**

6 tablespoons all-purpose flour

3 cups **low-sodium chicken broth**

1½ cups half-and-half

¾ teaspoon freshly ground black pepper

3 cups (12 ounces) shredded sharp white Cheddar

1 2½- to 3-pound **rotisserie chicken**, meat removed and shredded

Heat the oven to 375°F.

Bring a large pot of water to a boil and add 1 tablespoon salt. Add the vermicelli and cook, stirring until tender but still firm to the bite. Drain the vermicelli in a colander, but do not rinse.

In the same pot, melt the butter over medium-high heat. Add the onions and cook, stirring occasionally, until softened, about 5 minutes. Stir in the flour and cook for 1 minute. Slowly whisk in the broth and half-and-half. Add the remaining 1 teaspoon salt and the pepper. Bring to a boil, then reduce the heat to medium-low. Add the Cheddar and simmer, stirring frequently, until the cheese is melted. Add the chicken and vermicelli and stir to combine.

Pour the mixture into a 9 × 13-inch baking dish. Bake until the casserole is heated through, about 25 minutes. Remove the casserole from the oven. Let sit for 5 minutes before serving.

Chicken, Broccoli, and Rice Casserole

Mom believed in serving us homemade, balanced dinners. Every night we sat down to a meal with a protein, a "starch," and a green vegetable. If dinner was a casserole with meat and macaroni, you can bet that green beans or peas were served on the side. This casserole includes supermarket shortcuts from every category Mom insisted on—chicken, rice, and broccoli—so there's no need for a side. To this day, it remains my brother Chip's all-time favorite of Mom's. She still makes it for him every time he comes over for dinner.

MAKES 8 SERVINGS

1 2½- to 3-pound **rotisserie chicken**, meat removed and shredded

2 10.5-ounce cans **cream of broccoli soup**

2½ cups **low-sodium chicken broth**

2 8.8-ounce packages **Ben's Original Ready Rice**

1 16-ounce package **frozen broccoli florets**

2 cups (8 ounces) shredded sharp Cheddar

1 tablespoon onion powder

4 garlic cloves, minced

1½ teaspoons freshly ground black pepper

1 cup crushed **Ritz crackers**

Heat the oven to 350°F.

Put the chicken, soup, broth, rice, broccoli, cheese, onion powder, garlic, and pepper in a bowl. Stir well to combine. Pour the mixture into a 9 × 13-inch baking dish. Cover with aluminum foil and bake for 50 minutes. Remove the foil and sprinkle the cracker crumbs evenly on top. Return the casserole to the oven and bake until heated through and the topping is golden brown, about 15 minutes.

Chicken Teriyaki Casserole

Talk about a recipe that takes advantage of multiple supermarket shortcuts as well as the work out of prep work. Meat from a rotisserie chicken, stir-fry vegetables, and a few other ready-to-use ingredients are combined and baked. This colorful dish can be prepped ahead, refrigerated overnight, and then baked the next day.

MAKES 8 SERVINGS

1 2½- to 3-pound **rotisserie chicken**, meat removed and shredded

1 16-ounce package **frozen Asian stir-fry vegetable blend**

1 15-ounce can **baby corn**, drained

1 14.5-ounce bottle **thick teriyaki sauce**

1 8.8-ounce package **Ben's Original Ready Rice**

1 cup **low-sodium chicken broth**

1½ tablespoons minced fresh ginger

1 teaspoon freshly ground black pepper

1 20-ounce can **pineapple chunks**, drained well

1½ cups wonton crisps

Heat the oven to 375°F.

Put the chicken, vegetable blend, corn, teriyaki sauce, rice, broth, ginger, and pepper in a large bowl. Stir well to combine. Pour the mixture into a 9 × 13-inch baking dish. Cover with aluminum foil and bake for 30 minutes. Remove the foil and sprinkle the pineapple chunks evenly on top. Bake until heated through, about 20 minutes. Garnish with wonton crisps and serve.

Monte Cristo Casserole

Instead of making individual Monte Cristo sandwiches, fold pieces of ham, Swiss, and French bread into a mixture of eggs, half-and-half, and Dijon mustard. For color and just a hint of sweetness, strawberry jam is spooned on top before baking. Dust each portion with a snowy sprinkle of confectioners' sugar. Serve this colorful casserole for brunch, lunch, or dinner.

MAKES 8 SERVINGS

Vegetable oil spray

3 cups half-and-half

6 large eggs

3 tablespoons Dijon mustard

1 10-ounce baguette, cut into 1-inch pieces

1 pound deli ham, cut into 1-inch pieces

3 cups (12 ounces) shredded Swiss cheese

1 cup **strawberry jam**

1 teaspoon confectioners' sugar

Heat the oven to 350°F. Coat a 9 × 13-inch baking dish with vegetable oil spray.

Whisk together the half-and-half, eggs, and mustard in a large bowl. Using a spatula, fold in the baguette pieces, ham, and Swiss. Let the mixture sit for 10 minutes, until most of the liquid has been absorbed by the bread. Pour the mixture into the baking dish, pressing down firmly. Randomly dollop tablespoonsful of the jam on top.

Cover with aluminum foil and bake for 40 minutes. Remove the foil and continue to bake until golden brown on top and a knife inserted 2 inches from the edge of the baking dish comes out clean, 15 to 20 minutes. Remove the casserole from the oven and let rest for 5 minutes. Dust each serving with confectioners' sugar.

Summer Vegetable Gratin

This colorful dish goes well with beef, chicken, or seafood cooked on the grill. Uniformly thin slices of eggplant, zucchini, and tomatoes are layered, then blanketed with grated Parmigiano-Reggiano and Italian-flavored bread crumbs. The result is plenty of GBD—Golden Brown Deliciousness.

MAKES 8 TO 10 SERVINGS

½ cup **Italian seasoned bread crumbs**

1½ tablespoons extra-virgin olive oil

½ cup (1½ ounces) grated Parmigiano-Reggiano

1 pound eggplant, halved lengthwise, then into ¼-inch slices

¾ pound zucchini, cut into ¼-inch rounds

¾ pound yellow squash, cut into ¼-inch rounds

1 6.7-ounce jar **pesto**

1 teaspoon garlic salt

1 teaspoon freshly ground black pepper

1¼ pounds Roma tomatoes, quartered

Heat the oven to 375°F.

Combine the bread crumbs and olive oil in a bowl to coat. Stir in the Parmigiano-Reggiano. Set aside.

Put the eggplant, zucchini, yellow squash, pesto, garlic salt, and pepper in a bowl. Toss well to coat the vegetables. Layer the vegetables and the tomatoes in a 9 × 13-inch baking dish. Sprinkle the bread crumb mixture evenly on top. Cover with aluminum foil and bake for 30 minutes. Remove the foil and bake until the vegetables are tender and the crust is golden brown, 30 to 35 minutes.

CAST-IRON COOKING:

SIZZLE, SEAR, AND BAKE

There are so many reasons to invest in cast-iron cookware. You can sear, braise, roast, fry, and even bake in cast iron. Once a skillet or Dutch oven gets hot, it stays hot and uniformly distributes the heat so that food cooks evenly. The more you use your cast iron, the better it works. It lasts forever, unlike many nonstick pots and pans. Whether you choose enameled or non-enameled, today's cast-iron cookware is easy to clean.

Casseroles like Pizza Panade, Reuben "Sandwich" Skillet Bake, and Spaghetti Squash Alfredo go from the cooktop to the oven to the broiler to the table. (Cast iron is hot—use a trivet and wear kitchen mitts!) For sandwiches, Greek Grilled Cheese and Chicken Cordon Bleu Panini are crisp on the outside from the hot pan. You won't believe how much better your fried chicken tastes when cooked in a deep cast-iron Dutch oven. Even brookies, a combo of brownies and cookies baked beautifully and evenly in cast-iron. And the Skillet Mac 'n' Cheese . . . well, there are just no words.

Pizza Panade

A panade is part soup, part casserole. Torn chunks of bread, pizza sauce, sliced pepperoni, sausage, and lotsa mozzarella are combined in this scoopable one-skillet wonder. Personalize it with your favorite pizza toppings, like olives, onions, or mushrooms.

MAKES 8 SERVINGS

Vegetable oil

1 pound mild Italian sausage

1 16-ounce jar **pizza sauce**

1½ teaspoons **Italian seasoning**

1 16-ounce loaf rustic bread, cut into 1-inch chunks

4 garlic cloves, minced

1 green bell pepper, seeded and chopped

1 5-ounce bag **Pepperoni Minis**

2 cups (8 ounces) plus 2 cups (8 ounces) **shredded whole-milk mozzarella**

Heat the oven to 350°F. Lightly brush a large, deep cast-iron baking pan with vegetable oil.

Cook the sausage in the skillet over medium-high heat, breaking it into small pieces and stirring occasionally, until browned and cooked through, 6 to 8 minutes. Drain the sausage on a paper towel–lined plate.

Mix the pizza sauce and the Italian seasoning together in a bowl. Add the bread pieces and stir to coat completely. Toss in the garlic, bell pepper, cooked sausage, 1 cup Pepperoni Minis, and 2 cups mozzarella and combine well. Spoon the mixture into the prepared baking pan. Top with the remaining 2 cups mozzarella and Pepperoni Minis. Bake until heated through and the cheese melts, 40 to 45 minutes. Let rest for 5 minutes before serving.

Skillet Mac 'n' Cheese

Now, would I write a cookbook without a mac 'n' cheese recipe? No chance. My most favorite dish must have an ooey-gooey interior, a crispy top, and beautifully browned edges. What makes this one stand out is the blend of three cheeses, and it's cooked in a cast-iron skillet. That means it cooks evenly on the stovetop and can be safely put under the broiler to crisp and brown the top.

MAKES 8 SERVINGS

1 tablespoon kosher salt

1 pound medium shells

2 tablespoons unsalted butter

1 15-ounce jar **Cheez Whiz Original Cheese Dip**

1 cup (4 ounces) plus 1 cup (4 ounces) shredded extra-sharp Cheddar

1 cup (4 ounces) shredded American cheese

1 cup milk

1 teaspoon **Worcestershire sauce**

1 teaspoon freshly ground black pepper

Bring a large pot of water to a boil and add the salt. Add the shells and cook, stirring until tender but still firm to the bite. Reserve ¾ cup of the pasta cooking water, then drain the shells in a colander, but do not rinse.

Heat the oven to broil.

Melt the butter in a 12-inch cast-iron skillet over medium-low heat. Stir in the cheese dip, 1 cup Cheddar, the American cheese, milk, ¾ cup reserved pasta cooking water, Worcestershire, and pepper. Cook, stirring frequently, until the sauce is creamy and well blended, about 8 minutes. Add the shells to the pan and simmer, stirring frequently, until heated through. Sprinkle the remaining 1 cup Cheddar on top. Put the pan under the broiler and broil until the cheese is melted and slightly browned, 4 to 5 minutes. Let rest for 5 minutes before serving.

Easy Skillet Lasagna

One evening I was craving lasagna but didn't have the time to cook the noodles and layer it the traditional way. Instead, I combined broken-up noodles with a tomatoey, meaty sauce and some cheese and cooked the whole thing in a cast-iron skillet with a lid. If your skillet doesn't have a lid, just use one from another pot. Serve with a Caesar salad or some steamed broccoli.

MAKES 8 SERVINGS

1¼ cups (6 ounces) plus ¾ cup (3 ounces) **shredded whole-milk mozzarella**

1 cup whole-milk ricotta

⅓ cup plus ⅓ cup chopped fresh basil

¼ cup (¾ ounce) grated Parmigiano-Reggiano

2 teaspoons dried oregano leaves

½ teaspoon plus 1 teaspoon kosher salt

½ teaspoon plus ½ teaspoon freshly ground black pepper

1 pound lean ground beef

1 24-ounce jar **marinara sauce**

1 9-ounce box **oven-ready lasagna noodles**, broken into 2-inch pieces

Mix 1¼ cups mozzarella, the ricotta, ⅓ cup basil, Parmigiano-Reggiano, oregano, ½ teaspoon salt, and ½ teaspoon pepper in a bowl until combined.

Heat a large cast-iron skillet over medium-high heat. Add the beef and the remaining 1 teaspoon salt and ½ teaspoon pepper and cook, stirring frequently to break the beef into smaller pieces, until the meat is browned, 7 to 9 minutes.

Put the marinara sauce, 2 cups water, and broken noodles in a bowl. Mix until the noodles are thoroughly coated with the sauce, then add them to the skillet and stir. Reduce the heat to medium-low, cover, and simmer, stirring occasionally, until the noodles are tender, 25 to 30 minutes. Spoon dollops of the cheese mixture on top of the noodles and sprinkle with the remaining ¾ cup mozzarella. Cover and continue to cook until heated through and the cheese is melted, 10 to 15 minutes more. Let sit for 15 minutes before serving, garnished with the remaining ⅓ cup basil.

Reuben "Sandwich" Skillet Bake

Take me to a deli and you can bet that I'll order a Reuben sandwich. At home, I take those same ingredients—deli corned beef, Swiss cheese, sauerkraut, and Thousand Island dressing—and add a twist. Instead of bread, I bake them on a bed of hash brown potatoes in a cast-iron skillet and use caraway seeds to give the dish that rye bread flavor. Serve with coleslaw and dill pickles for a true deli experience.

MAKES 6 SERVINGS

---

4 cups **diced hash brown potatoes**, thawed

2 tablespoons vegetable oil

¾ teaspoon plus ¾ teaspoon caraway seeds

½ teaspoon kosher salt

½ teaspoon freshly ground black pepper

1 pound **sliced corned beef**, cut into 1-inch pieces

1 14.5-ounce can **sauerkraut**, rinsed and drained well

1 cup **Thousand Island dressing**

2 cups (8 ounces) shredded Swiss cheese

Heat the oven to 400°F.

Put the potatoes, oil, ¾ teaspoon caraway seeds, salt, and pepper in a bowl. Stir well to combine. Spread the potatoes evenly in a large cast-iron skillet. Bake until the potatoes are heated through, about 25 minutes.

Layer the corned beef, followed by sauerkraut, over the potatoes. Drizzle with the Thousand Island dressing. Sprinkle the Swiss cheese and the remaining ¾ teaspoon caraway seeds evenly on top. Bake until heated through, 15 to 20 minutes. Let sit for 5 minutes before serving.

Cast-Iron Fried Chicken

Some Sundays, once we got home from church and changed out of our "good" clothes, Mom would put on her apron and make fried chicken. She cut up a whole chicken and dredged the pieces in milk and seasoned flour. Then she fried the parts in a cast-iron skillet. Mom says, "Fried chicken cooked in any other pan never tastes as good." I put my own spin on her version by adding more seasonings and using a large cast-iron Dutch oven. The method below results in juicy meat and a crispy crust. I know this recipe will make Mom proud.

MAKES 4 TO 6 SERVINGS

2 cups buttermilk

1 tablespoon plus 1 teaspoon garlic salt

2 teaspoons plus 1½ teaspoons freshly ground black pepper

1 3½- to 4-pound chicken, cut into 8 pieces (2 breasts, each halved, 2 thighs, and 2 drumsticks)

1¼ cups all-purpose flour

2 tablespoons **Lawry's Seasoned Salt**

2 tablespoons **Italian seasoning**

1 tablespoon onion powder

2 teaspoons baking powder

Vegetable oil for frying

Mix the buttermilk, 1 tablespoon garlic salt, and 2 teaspoons pepper in a large resealable plastic bag. Put the chicken pieces in the bag. Put the bag in a shallow dish so the pieces lie flat. Refrigerate overnight.

Combine the flour, seasoned salt, Italian seasoning, onion powder, baking powder, the remaining 1 teaspoon garlic salt, and 1½ teaspoons pepper in a shallow bowl.

Line a sheet pan with parchment paper and place a wire rack on top. Remove the chicken from the marinade and discard the liquid. Dredge the chicken pieces in the flour mixture, firmly pressing the flour into each piece without shaking off any excess. Place the dredged pieces on the wire rack and refrigerate, uncovered, for 1 hour.

Clip a deep-frying thermometer to the side of a cast-iron Dutch oven. Add 1½ inches of oil and slowly heat it to 350°F. Place the chicken pieces, skin side down, into the hot oil. The pieces can overlap slightly. Remove the thermometer, cover with the lid, and cook for 10 minutes. Remove the lid and turn the chicken pieces over. Cook the chicken, uncovered, for an additional 10 to 12 minutes. The chicken is done when an instant-read thermometer inserted into the thickest parts, but not touching the bone, registers 165°F. Remove the chicken to a wire rack set over paper towels. Let drain and rest 5 minutes before serving.

Chicken Cordon Bleu Panini

Slices of rustic bread are layered with thinly sliced chicken, Canadian bacon, and Swiss cheese, then smeared with garlic-and-herbs cheese spread and mustard. Grill it in a cast-iron skillet. If you don't have a weighted sandwich press, wrap the outside of another cast-iron skillet with aluminum foil to use as a weight. Serve with soup. Then go ahead and dip your sandwich into your soup.

MAKES 2 SERVINGS

⅓ cup **garlic-and-herbs spreadable cheese**

3 tablespoons grated Parmigiano-Reggiano

2½ tablespoons Dijon mustard

¾ teaspoon **Italian seasoning**

¾ teaspoon onion powder

4 slices rustic bread

8 slices Swiss cheese

6 slices Canadian bacon

12 thin **slices cooked chicken breast**

Using a spatula, mix together the spreadable cheese, Parmigiano-Reggiano, Dijon, Italian seasoning, and onion powder in a bowl.

Heat a ridged grill pan over medium heat.

Spread a fourth of the cheese mixture on each slice of bread. On 2 slices, layer, in the following order, 2 slices Swiss cheese, 3 slices Canadian bacon, 6 slices chicken, and 2 slices Swiss cheese. Top with the remaining 2 bread slices. Grill the sandwiches, using a press, until the bread is golden brown, the meat is heated through, and the cheese is melted, about 10 minutes, turning the sandwiches once during the cooking process. Serve hot.

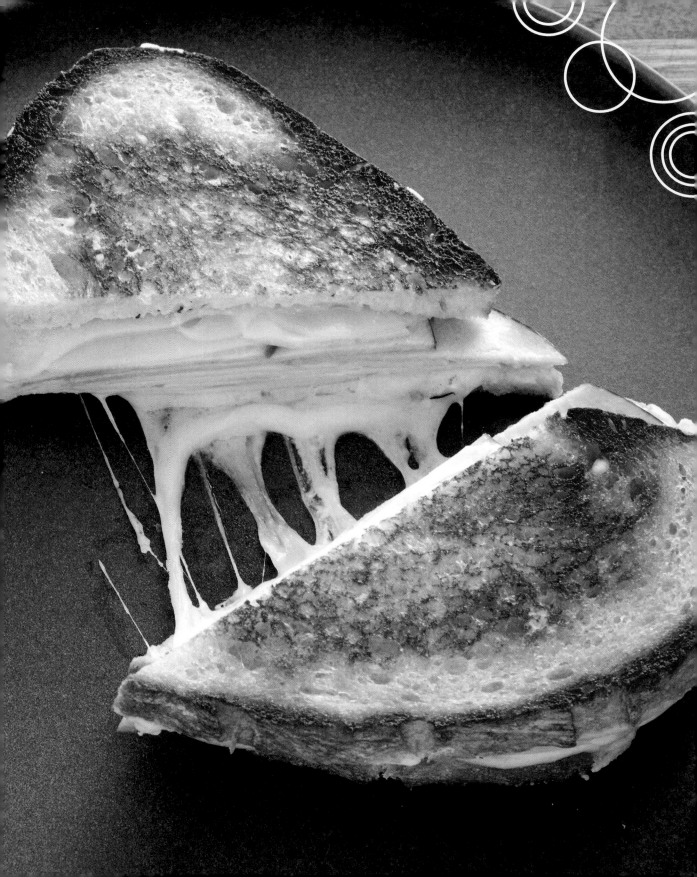

Greek Grilled Cheese Sandwiches

Hector's in Chapel Hill was the go-to place for me and my UNC college buddies after a late night on the town. Now closed, it was known for its double cheeseburgers on pita and this one-of-a-kind sandwich: mozzarella and feta cheeses, vegetables, and tzatziki piled between two pitas and grilled until hot and gooey. Who says you can't go home again?

MAKES 2 SERVINGS

1 cup (4 ounces) **shredded whole-milk mozzarella**

3 tablespoons **feta crumbles**

⅓ cup chopped fresh baby spinach leaves

2 tablespoons drained and chopped **roasted red peppers**

⅛ cup **chopped red onions**

1 pepperoncini, seeded and chopped

⅛ teaspoon freshly ground black pepper

2 tablespoons **tzatziki**

2 pitas

Heat a cast-iron skillet over medium heat.

Put the mozzarella, feta, spinach, red peppers, onions, pepperoncini, and black pepper in a bowl. Stir to combine.

Put the cheese mixture and tzatziki sauce on 1 pita round. Top with the remaining pita and place it in the skillet. Grill until the bread is golden brown and the cheese mixture is heated through and melted, 8 to 10 minutes, turning the sandwich halfway through cooking. Cut the sandwich in half to make 2 servings.

Spaghetti Squash Alfredo

When cooked, the flesh of this vegetable separates into golden strands that look just like spaghetti. Also like pasta, spaghetti squash serves as a blank canvas when combined with other ingredients. Toss it with jarred Alfredo sauce, mozzarella, and lots of cooked bacon pieces, then twirl it on your fork.

MAKES 6 TO 8 SERVINGS

1 3-pound spaghetti squash, halved lengthwise, seeds removed

1 pound sliced bacon, cut into 1-inch pieces

1 15-ounce jar **Alfredo sauce**

2 cups (8 ounces) plus 1 cup (4 ounces) **shredded whole-milk mozzarella**

½ cup plus ¼ cup chopped fresh basil

6 garlic cloves, minced

1 teaspoon freshly ground black pepper

½ cup (1½ ounces) grated Parmigiano-Reggiano

Heat the oven to 350°F. Line a sheet pan with parchment paper. Put the spaghetti squash halves, cut side down, on the sheet pan. Bake until tender when pierced with a fork, 45 to 50 minutes.

While the squash is baking, cook the bacon in a 12-inch cast-iron skillet over medium heat until crisp, about 20 minutes. Using a slotted spoon, remove the bacon to a paper towel-lined plate. Put 2 tablespoons of the bacon fat in a bowl and discard the rest. Add the Alfredo sauce, 2 cups mozzarella, ½ cup basil, the garlic, pepper, and half of the cooked bacon to the bowl and mix.

When done, remove the squash from the oven. Carefully turn them cut side up and cool for 10 minutes. Using a fork, scrape and fluff the strands from the sides of the squash, add it to the bowl with the other ingredients, and mix well.

Pour the squash mixture into the skillet with the bacon fat. Sprinkle on the Parmigiano-Reggiano and the remaining 1 cup mozzarella, ¼ cup basil, and bacon. Bake until the cheese is melted and the squash is bubbling around the edges, 30 to 35 minutes. Let sit for 5 minutes before serving.

Turtle Brookies

Is it a brownie? Or a cookie? The answers are yes and yes. Have the best of both worlds in this indulgent combination of chocolate chip cookies and fudgy brownies. These bars are put together using a brownie mix and chocolate chip cookie mix and baked in a cast-iron skillet. They're best eaten warm. A scoop of ice cream—maybe vanilla or salted caramel— is always welcome.

MAKES 12 SERVINGS

½ cup vegetable oil, plus more for the skillet

1 20-ounce box **brownie mix**

1 large egg plus 1 large egg

1¼ teaspoons **instant espresso coffee granules**

½ cup chopped walnuts, toasted

9 plus 9 soft caramels

1 17.5-oz bag **chocolate chip cookie mix**

½ cup (1 stick) unsalted butter, at room temperature

Heat the oven to 350°F. Lightly brush a 12-inch cast-iron skillet with vegetable oil.

Put the brownie mix, oil, 1 egg, instant espresso, and ¼ cup water in the bowl of an electric mixer. Beat on medium speed just until combined. Using a spatula, fold the walnuts into the batter. Scrape the batter into the prepared skillet. (Scrape well, so there's no need to wash the bowl to make the cookies.) Arrange 9 of the caramels on top, avoiding the edges of the skillet.

Put the cookie mix, butter, and the remaining egg in the bowl of an electric mixer. Beat on medium just until combined. Since the cookie dough is too thick to spread, flatten about ¼ cup dough with your hands and place it on top of the brownie mix, leaving a 1½-inch rim around the edge of the pan. Continue until the remaining dough is used. Arrange the remaining 9 caramels on top of the cookie dough, avoiding the edges of the skillet.

Bake until golden brown and a toothpick inserted in several places comes out with just a few crumbs, 40 to 45 minutes. Remove from the oven and allow to cool on a wire rack before slicing into wedges.

SIDES:

PERFECT PARTNERS

Many foods have natural perfect partners. Peanut butter and jelly. Cream cheese and bagels. Grilled cheese and tomato soup. Here you'll find new ideas for main dish partners. Slow Cooker Pork Stew definitely needs some Smashed Potatoes with Pancetta and Gorgonzola so no gravy is left behind. A simple roast chicken yearns for a side of Green Beans, Red Onions, and Crisp Chickpeas. Oven-Baked Baby Back Ribs beg for a bowl of Creamy Off the Cob Corn. Herb-Roasted Turkey Breast has found its mate in Acorn Squash Wedges with Cranberries and Almonds. Food-friendly Sheet Pan Roasted Vegetables go with everything from Cedar-Planked Grilled Salmon to tuna, turkey, and beef burgers.

Have fun finding the perfect partners for your favorite dishes.

Acorn Squash Wedges with Cranberries and Almonds

Dark green and ridged on the outside, the flesh of acorn squash is yellow orange with a sweet, nutty, and buttery flavor. These roasted wedges with their warm filling make colorful partners to roast chicken, turkey, or pork any time of the year.

MAKES 8 SERVINGS

2 acorn squash

1 tablespoon extra-virgin olive oil

½ teaspoon kosher salt

¼ teaspoon freshly ground black pepper

⅔ cup **orange marmalade**

⅓ cup **dried cranberries**

¼ cup sliced almonds

2 tablespoons unsalted butter

¼ teaspoon ground cinnamon

1½ tablespoons chopped fresh flat-leaf parsley leaves

Heat the oven to 375°F. Line a sheet pan with aluminum foil.

Cut the acorn squash in half and scrape out the seeds with a spoon. Cut each in half for a total of 8 wedges. Brush the wedges with the oil and sprinkle them with the salt and pepper. Put the wedges, cut side up, on the prepared sheet pan. Bake until tender and cooked through, 50 to 55 minutes.

Whisk together the marmalade, cranberries, almonds, butter, and cinnamon in a saucepan over medium heat. Cook until bubbly, about 4 minutes, then stir in the parsley. Spoon the mixture over the warm squash wedges before serving.

Sheet Pan Roasted Vegetables

Keep these roasted vegetables on hand to add beautiful splashes of color to meals throughout the week. Enjoy them as a side, atop salad greens, or to accompany grilled chicken, fish, or steak. Toss with pasta and tomato sauce. Pile them on a slice of rustic bread, top with mozzarella, and quickly pass it under the broiler for an open-faced sandwich. For evenly cooked vegetables, cut them into pieces of similar size.

MAKES 8 SERVINGS

1 pound zucchini, halved horizontally, then into 1-inch slices

½ pound yellow squash, halved horizontally, then into 1-inch slices

1 red bell pepper, seeded and cut into 1-inch strips

1 yellow bell pepper, seeded and cut into 1-inch strips

1 medium red onion, cut into ½-inch wedges

2 8-ounce packages of mushrooms

⅓ cup extra-virgin olive oil

2 0.27-ounce package **balsamic dressing & recipe mix**

¾ teaspoon freshly ground black pepper

Heat the oven to 400°F. Line a sheet pan with aluminum foil.

Put the zucchini, squash, bell peppers, red onion, mushrooms, olive oil, balsamic dressing mix, and pepper in a large bowl and toss to coat. Arrange the vegetables in a single layer on the prepared sheet pan. Roast until the vegetables are brown on the outside and tender on the inside when pierced with a knife, 35 to 40 minutes.

Green Beans, Red Onions, and Crisp Chickpeas

Green beans are one of my favorite vegetables, and I love discovering new ways to prepare them. Oven roasting green beans and red onions with spices deepens their flavors. Just before serving, add some roasted chickpeas from a pouch for some crunch.

MAKES 8 SERVINGS

2 pounds green beans, trimmed

1 cup **thinly sliced red onions**

2 tablespoons extra-virgin olive oil

6 garlic cloves, thinly sliced

1½ teaspoons ground cumin

1 teaspoon smoked paprika

1 teaspoon dried oregano

1 teaspoon kosher salt

1 teaspoon freshly ground black pepper

1 cup packaged **sea salt chickpeas**

Heat the oven to 375°F. Line a sheet pan with aluminum foil.

Put the green beans, red onions, olive oil, garlic, cumin, smoked paprika, oregano, salt, and pepper in a bowl and toss to coat. Arrange the green bean mixture in a single layer on the prepared sheet pan. Bake until the green beans are tender and cooked through, 35 to 40 minutes. Put the green bean mixture in a bowl and stir in the chickpeas. Serve warm.

Creamy Corn off the Cob

When corn and cream cheese are partnered with other vegetables, they become one rich, velvety side dish. A hint of jalapeño adds just a little zip. Serve this creamy, tomatoey combo with anything cooked on the grill, like shrimp, chicken, or pork chops.

MAKES 6 SERVINGS

2 tablespoons unsalted butter

1 cup **chopped yellow onions**

1 red bell pepper, seeded and chopped

1 16-ounce package **frozen corn kernels**, thawed

1 10-ounce can **RO*TEL Diced Tomatoes and Green Chilies**

1 8-ounce package cream cheese

2 to 3 tablespoons chopped jalapeño peppers, seeds and membranes removed

1 teaspoon kosher salt

1 teaspoon freshly ground black pepper

2 tablespoons chopped fresh flat-leaf parsley leaves

Melt the butter in a large skillet over medium-high heat. Add the onions and bell peppers and cook, stirring frequently, until the vegetables are softened, 7 to 9 minutes.

Add the corn, diced tomatoes and chilies, cream cheese, jalapeños, salt, and pepper to the skillet. Stir the mixture to combine. Reduce the heat to medium and cook, stirring occasionally, until the corn mixture is heated through, about 10 minutes. Stir in the parsley just before serving.

Spinach Pie

This smooth and savory crustless pie goes well with grilled steak, seafood, or chicken. Whisk all the ingredients together and bake it in a pie dish, and you have a great alternative to traditional steak-house-style creamed spinach. This dish will dress up your lunch or brunch table.

MAKES 8 TO 10 SERVINGS

Vegetable oil spray

8 large eggs

¾ cup milk

⅓ cup (1 ounce) grated Asiago

¾ teaspoon freshly ground black pepper

½ teaspoon kosher salt

3 garlic cloves, minced

1 16-ounce package **frozen chopped spinach**, thawed and well drained

¾ cup cottage cheese

½ cup chopped **roasted red peppers**, well drained

Heat the oven to 350°F. Lightly coat a 9-inch round deep pie dish with vegetable oil spray.

In a bowl, whisk the eggs, milk, Asiago, black pepper, salt, and garlic until blended, about 1 minute. Add the spinach, cottage cheese, and roasted red peppers and mix until combined. Pour the mixture into the prepared pie dish. Bake for 60 to 65 minutes, until the filling is set and golden brown on the edges. Let rest 5 minutes before cutting into wedges and serving.

Scalloped Potatoes with Smoked Gouda

The secret to tender and evenly cooked scalloped potatoes is to make sure that the sliced potatoes and onions are all the same thickness. A mandoline is the best kitchen tool for this task. Smoked Gouda lends a delicate woodsy flavor to the dish. This rich and cheesy gratin stands up to roast beef, pork chops, and grilled steaks.

MAKES 8 TO 10 SERVINGS

Vegetable oil spray

3 pounds Yukon gold potatoes, unpeeled and sliced ¼-inch thick

1½ teaspoons kosher salt, divided

1½ teaspoons freshly ground black pepper, divided

1½ teaspoons **Italian seasoning**, divided

3 tablespoons minced garlic

2¼ cups **thinly sliced yellow onions**, divided

2¼ cups (9 ounces) shredded smoked Gouda, divided

3¾ cups (30 ounces) heavy cream, divided

2 tablespoons chopped fresh flat-leaf parsley leaves

Heat the oven to 350°F. Coat a 9 × 13-inch baking dish with vegetable oil spray.

Arrange a third of the sliced potatoes on the bottom of the prepared baking dish. Sprinkle the potatoes with ½ teaspoon salt, ½ teaspoon pepper, ½ teaspoon Italian seasoning, and 1 tablespoon garlic. Evenly sprinkle ¾ cup onions and ¾ cup smoked Gouda on top. Pour 1¼ cups heavy cream evenly on top of the potatoes. Repeat twice, making 2 more layers.

Cover the baking dish with aluminum foil and bake for 30 minutes. Remove the foil and bake until the potatoes can be pierced with a fork and are lightly browned on top, 45 to 55 minutes. Let rest 10 minutes. Garnish with the parsley before serving.

Smashed Potatoes with Pancetta and Gorgonzola

This decadent side is loaded with flavor and textures. Small squares of crispy pancetta and bits of smooth Gorgonzola are combined with chunky potatoes. A dish this rich and impressive deserves to be partnered with roast chicken for Sunday supper or ham for a holiday dinner.

MAKES 4 TO 6 SERVINGS

1 4-ounce package **diced pancetta**

1½ pounds russet potatoes, peeled and cut into 2-inch pieces

1 teaspoon plus ¼ teaspoon kosher salt

¾ cup half-and-half

⅓ cup plus ¼ cup **Gorgonzola crumbles**

½ teaspoon freshly ground black pepper

1 tablespoon chopped fresh chives

Put the pancetta in a skillet over medium-high heat. Cook, stirring occasionally, until crisp, 12 to 15 minutes. Using a slotting spoon, remove the pancetta to a plate. Measure 1½ tablespoons fat, set it aside, and discard the rest.

Put the potatoes and 1 teaspoon salt a large pot. Add cold water to cover the potatoes by 1 inch. Bring to a boil, reduce the heat to medium, and simmer until the potatoes can be pierced with a fork, 15 to 20 minutes. Drain the potatoes in a colander, then put them in the bowl of an electric mixer.

Add the half-and-half, ⅓ cup Gorgonzola, 1½ tablespoons reserved pancetta fat, pepper, ¼ teaspoon salt, and half the pancetta. Beat the potatoes on low speed just until the ingredients are combined, 35 to 45 seconds. (You can also use a handheld mixer.) The potatoes should be a bit chunky, not completely smooth. Before serving, top with the remaining pancetta and ¼ cup Gorgonzola and the chives. Serve hot.

Sweet Potatoes with Pecan Streusel

Instead of whole marshmallows baked on top, marshmallow crème is combined with the mashed sweets to put a new spin on a traditional favorite. It's topped with a crunchy pecan streusel. Serve during the festive holiday season or partner with roast beef or chicken any time of the year.

MAKES 8 TO 10 SERVINGS

1 cup chopped pecans

1 cup all-purpose flour

¾ cup (packed) light brown sugar

6 tablespoons (¾ stick) unsalted butter, melted

1 tablespoon ground cinnamon

¼ teaspoon plus 1 tablespoon plus ½ teaspoon kosher salt

4 pounds **sweet potatoes, peeled and cut into 1-inch pieces**

¾ cup **marshmallow crème**

¾ cup whole milk

¼ teaspoon freshly ground black pepper

Heat the oven to 350°F.

Put the pecans, flour, brown sugar, butter, cinnamon, and ¼ teaspoon salt in a bowl. Mix until combined and crumbly. Set the streusel aside.

Put the sweet potatoes and 1 tablespoon salt in a large pot. Add cold water to cover the potatoes by 1 inch. Bring to a boil and reduce the heat to medium. Simmer until the potatoes can be pierced with a fork, 15 to 20 minutes. Drain the potatoes in a colander and put them in the bowl of an electric mixer.

Add the marshmallow crème, milk, pepper, and the remaining ½ teaspoon salt to the potatoes. Beat the potatoes on low speed until the potatoes are mashed and smooth, about 1 minute. (You can also use a handheld mixer.)

Spoon the sweet potato mixture into a 9 × 13-inch baking dish. Sprinkle the streusel evenly on top. Bake until heated through and the streusel is golden brown, 35 to 40 minutes.

BREADS & MORE:

BAKE YOU HAPPY

Baking fresh-from-the-oven goodies uses all of your senses. See yeast do its magic as the Yeasted Dinner Rolls rise. Taste the moist crumb of Chocolate Chip–Banana Bread. Hear the sighs of happiness as guests take their first bites of homemade baked goods. Smell the warming aroma of Cathead Biscuits while they bake. Feel the tender and springy Focaccia dough as you press it into a pan.

If this is your first time baking with yeast, you'll soon discover how easy and rewarding the process is. Once the dough is put together, you set it aside and wait for it to rise as the bakery aromas travel throughout your home.

The others—muffins, cheese bread, biscuits, and loaves—fall into the quick bread category, which means baking soda and baking powder make them rise. I've eaten a lot of banana bread in my day, but this version with chocolate chips takes the cake. For a savory loaf, slice and serve the Ham and Cheese Quick Bread as an appetizer, in place of a sandwich, or with a bowl of soup.

If you don't want to spend a lot of time baking, try the Donut Bread Pudding. It's made with store-bought glazed donuts, covered with an egg-and-milk mixture and raspberry jam, and then baked. Each bite offers sweet creaminess and a pop of fruity goodness.

Cathead Biscuits

Legend has it that these are called cathead biscuits because, well, each one is the size of a cat's head. Any butter lovers out there? Butter is a triple treat in these light and airy biscuits. It's used to grease the cast-iron skillet. Frozen cubes of butter and butter-flavored shortening give these biscuits flaky tenderness. Finally, melted butter is brushed on the tops just before baking. While a cast-iron skillet evenly bakes these savory delights, be sure to remove them from the pan after a few minutes so they don't overbake.

MAKES 8

1 tablespoon plus 2 tablespoons unsalted butter, melted

3½ cups all-purpose flour, plus more for rolling

3 tablespoons sugar

5½ teaspoons baking powder

2½ teaspoons kosher salt

1 teaspoon baking soda

⅓ cup butter-flavored vegetable shortening, cut into ½-inch pieces and frozen

¼ cup (½ stick) unsalted butter, cut into ¼-inch pieces and frozen

1⅔ cups buttermilk

Coat a 12-inch cast-iron skillet with 1 tablespoon melted butter. Heat the oven to 425°F.

Put the flour, sugar, baking powder, salt, and baking soda in a food processor and pulse until mixed. Add the frozen shortening and frozen butter and pulse until the dough is the texture of coarse sand, 8 to 10 pulses. Put the flour mixture into a bowl, pour in the buttermilk, and mix with a spatula until it just comes together. The dough will be sticky and pieces of the butter and shortening will be visible.

Put the dough on a lightly floured surface, press it together, and flatten it with your hands into a 1¼-inch-thick disk. Cut the biscuits using a 3-inch biscuit cutter. Arrange the biscuits in the prepared skillet and brush the tops with the remaining 2 tablespoons melted butter. Bake for 20 minutes, until light golden brown on top. Overbaking will result in dry, crumbly biscuits. Remove from the oven and let the biscuits sit in the skillet for 5 minutes. Put them in a napkin-lined basket and serve.

Brazilian Cheese Bread

When a friend served these at a dinner party, it was all I could do to let the other guests enjoy them as well. When my pal noticed how much I liked them, he sent me home with the leftovers. Gluten-free tapioca flour can easily be found in supermarket baking sections. These chewy individual rolls are called bread in Brazil and are best served warm right from the oven.

MAKES 10

⅓ cup whole milk

5 tablespoons vegetable oil

1 teaspoon kosher salt

2 cups tapioca flour

2 large eggs

¾ cup (2¼ ounces) grated Parmigiano-Reggiano

1¼ cups (6 ounces) **part-skim, low-moisture shredded mozzarella**

Heat the oven to 375°F. Line a sheet pan with parchment paper.

Heat the milk, oil, salt, and ⅓ cup water in a saucepan over medium-high heat. Once the mixture comes to a boil, remove it from the heat and stir in the tapioca flour until smooth. Put the dough into the bowl of an electric mixer and beat for 2 to 3 minutes to cool slightly. Add the eggs, one at a time, until incorporated. Add the cheeses and beat just to mix. The dough will be sticky and lumpy.

Dip a ¼-cup measure into hot water, then scoop the batter onto the prepared sheet pan about 2 inches apart. For easy release, dip the measure into hot water before each scoop. Bake until lightly browned, 32 to 34 minutes. Serve warm.

Yeasted Dinner Rolls

Flaky. Buttery. Heavenly. These rolls are so light and fluffy they almost float off the table. Pass a napkin-lined basket of these tender rolls at any dinner party. They're also sturdy enough to make sandwiches with leftover Oven-Baked Brisket (page 104) or Slow Cooker Shredded Beef (page 103).

MAKES 9

2½ cups all-purpose flour

1 0.25-ounce envelope active dry yeast

3½ tablespoons sugar

¾ teaspoon plus ⅛ teaspoon kosher salt

¾ cup warm (120°F to 130°F) milk

1 large egg

3 tablespoons plus 3 tablespoons unsalted butter, at room temperature

Vegetable oil spray

Put the flour, yeast, sugar, ¾ teaspoon salt, warm milk, egg, and 3 tablespoons butter in the bowl of an electric mixer with the dough hook. Beat on medium speed until the dough pulls away from the sides and forms a ball, 4 to 5 minutes.

Coat a large bowl with vegetable oil spray. Put the dough into the bowl and roll it around to coat the entire ball with oil. Cover with plastic wrap and let rise in a warm place for 1 hour.

Coat a 9 × 9-inch baking pan with vegetable oil spray. Punch down the dough and divide it into 9 equal-size pieces. Using your hands, roll each piece into a ball and place into the prepared pan. Cover the pan with plastic wrap and let rise in a warm place until doubled in size, about 1 hour 20 minutes.

Heat the oven to 350°F. Remove the plastic wrap. Bake until cooked through and golden brown on top, 20 to 22 minutes. Remove the pan from the oven and place it on a wire rack.

Melt the remaining 3 tablespoons butter and brush it all over the rolls. Sprinkle on the remaining ⅛ teaspoon salt. Serve warm.

Focaccia

While Italian focaccia and pizza are both flat and oven baked, focaccia is generously drizzled with olive oil and maybe some herbs. If you've been reluctant to try baking bread, this easy recipe is definitely the one to start with. Enjoy warm squares with soups and salads, as sandwich bread, or even as an appetizer with a glass of wine.

MAKES 10 TO 12 SERVINGS

5⅓ cups unbleached bread flour

2 0.25-ounce envelopes active dry yeast

1 tablespoon plus 1½ teaspoons kosher salt

1½ tablespoons **Italian seasoning**

1½ tablespoons garlic powder

1 tablespoon dried parsley flakes

2 cups warm water (120°F to 130°F)

5 tablespoons plus 1 tablespoon plus 1½ tablespoons plus 1½ tablespoons extra-virgin olive oil

Put the flour, yeast, 1 tablespoon salt, Italian seasoning, garlic powder, parsley flakes, warm water, and 5 tablespoons olive oil in the bowl of an electric mixer. Using the dough hook attachment, mix on medium speed until the dough comes together, then continue kneading the dough for an additional 6 to 7 minutes. Shape the dough into a ball.

Coat the sides of a large bowl with 1 tablespoon olive oil. Put the dough ball in the bowl and roll it around to coat the whole thing with oil. Cover with plastic wrap and refrigerate for at least 10 hours or overnight.

Coat a sheet pan with 1½ tablespoons olive oil. Put the dough onto the pan, coating it with oil, then flip the dough to coat the other side. Stretch the dough to fit in the pan. Using your fingertips, poke holes through the dough to give the focaccia its characteristic dimpled look. Cover with plastic wrap, put in a warm place, and let rise until doubled in size, 1½ to 2 hours.

Position a rack in the center of the oven and heat to 400°F. Remove the plastic wrap. Drizzle the dough with the remaining 1½ tablespoons olive oil, then sprinkle the dough with the remaining 1½ teaspoons salt. Bake until light golden brown, 24 to 28 minutes. Remove from the oven and cool in the pan on a wire rack for 5 minutes before cutting it into pieces. Focaccia is best served warm.

Ham and Cheese Quick Bread

In France, a savory quick bread is called cake salé, which translates as "salty cake" (salty here means savory). Serve this delicious loaf the same day you bake it. Offer slices of this easy-to-put-together bread for brunch, with a glass of wine before a meal, or alongside a salad. I like to toast cubes and float them in tomato or other creamy soups.

MAKES 8 SERVINGS

⅓ cup extra-virgin olive oil, plus more for the pan

1⅓ cups all-purpose flour, plus more for the pan

2 ¼ teaspoons baking powder

1 teaspoon freshly ground black pepper

½ teaspoon kosher salt

4 large eggs

½ cup buttermilk

¼ cup fresh chopped flat-leaf parsley leaves

1 4-ounce package **sliced prosciutto**, chopped

1⅓ cups (4 ounces) shredded Asiago

Heat the oven to 350°F. Grease and flour a 5 × 9-inch loaf pan.

Whisk the flour, baking powder, pepper, and salt together in a bowl. Set aside.

Whisk the eggs, buttermilk, olive oil, and parsley together in a bowl. Add the flour mixture to the wet ingredients and stir just until combined. Using a spatula, fold the prosciutto and cheese into the batter. Pour the batter evenly into the prepared pan. Bake until a toothpick inserted in several places comes out clean, 35 to 40 minutes. Remove from the oven and let cool on a wire rack for 20 minutes. Invert cake onto a serving plate and slice to serve.

Rolled Cinnamon-Cream Cheese Muffins

Turn a can of cinnamon rolls into muffins without making a batter. Just roll the dough into a log and slice into twelve rounds that fit into a muffin pan. Add a layer of a cheesecake filling, then top with a streusel. Once baked, spoon the icing onto the hot muffins.

MAKES 12 SERVINGS

Vegetable oil spray

¼ cup (packed) light brown sugar

3 tablespoons plus ¼ cup granulated sugar

1½ teaspoons plus ½ teaspoon ground cinnamon

⅛ teaspoon kosher salt

4 tablespoons (½ stick) unsalted butter, melted

¾ cup all-purpose flour

1 12.4-ounce can refrigerated **cinnamon rolls with icing**

1 8-ounce package cream cheese, at room temperature

1 large egg

Heat the oven to 350°F. Spray a standard 12-cup muffin pan with vegetable oil spray.

Combine the brown sugar, 3 tablespoons granulated sugar, 1½ teaspoons cinnamon, and salt in a bowl. Stir in the butter to combine. Add the flour and, using clean hands, mix until crumbs form. Set the streusel aside.

Remove the cinnamon rolls from the can and stack them on top of each other. Using your hands, firmly press down on the stack and flatten it into a 1-inch-thick disk. Roll it up again into a log about 1½ inches in diameter. Slice the log into 12 rounds. Place one round into each of the 12 prepared muffin pan cups. Sprinkle the rounds with the remaining ½ teaspoon cinnamon.

Put the cream cheese, the remaining ¼ cup granulated sugar, and the egg in the bowl of an electric mixer. Beat until creamy, 2 to 3 minutes. Spoon about 2 tablespoons of the filling onto each round. Sprinkle the streusel evenly over the cream cheese filling.

Bake until light golden brown on top, 15 to 17 minutes. Remove the pan from the oven and cool on a wire rack for 5 minutes. Place the muffins on a plate and drizzle on the icing.

Chocolate Chip–Banana Bread

The secret to making super-moist banana bread is all about the bananas. The riper the bananas, the sweeter and better your bread will be. I also like to stir in a handful of chocolate chips to give it another flavor layer. Like wine, this loaf gets better with time. Wrap well in plastic and it will keep for five days ... if you're lucky.

MAKES 8 TO 10 SERVINGS

Vegetable oil spray

1⅓ cups sugar

4 ripe bananas, 3 mashed and 1 sliced into ¼-inch pieces

½ cup vegetable oil

2 large eggs

2 teaspoons pure vanilla extract

2 cups all-purpose flour

1 teaspoon baking soda

½ teaspoon kosher salt

½ cup semisweet chocolate chips

Heat the oven to 350°F. Coat a 5 × 9-inch loaf pan with vegetable oil spray.

Stir together the sugar, 3 mashed bananas, and oil in a bowl. Whisk in the eggs and vanilla, then mix in the flour, baking soda, and salt just until combined. Do not overmix. Gently fold in the banana slices and chocolate chips. Pour the batter evenly into the prepared pan.

Bake until a toothpick inserted in several places comes out with just a few crumbs, 70 to 80 minutes. Remove the pan from the oven and let cool on a wire rack for 50 minutes. Invert the bread onto a serving plate and let cool completely before slicing.

Donut Bread Pudding

When Mom said that, if we all hurried, we could stop for donuts on the way to Sunday church, you've never seen three kids dress so quickly. I always chose a jelly donut with its sweet center, tender dough, and glazed-sugar topping. For this treat, cut-up store-bought glazed donuts are mixed with milk and eggs before baking. To take this truly over the top, enjoy warm with a scoop of vanilla ice cream.

MAKES 8 SERVINGS

Vegetable oil spray

2½ cups plus 2½ tablespoons half-and-half

5 large eggs

¼ cup granulated sugar

4 tablespoons (½ stick) plus 2 tablespoons (¼ stick) unsalted butter, melted

1 tablespoon pure vanilla extract

½ teaspoon kosher salt

12 **glazed donuts**, quartered

½ cup **seedless raspberry jam**

1 cup confectioners' sugar

Heat the oven to 350°F. Coat a 9 × 13-inch baking dish with vegetable oil spray.

Whisk together 2½ cups half-and-half, the eggs, granulated sugar, 4 tablespoons melted butter, the vanilla, and salt in a bowl. Add the donut pieces and toss gently to combine. Pour the mixture evenly into the prepared dish. Spoon the jam randomly all over the top. Bake until golden brown and the custard is set, 40 to 45 minutes.

Whisk together the remaining 2½ tablespoons half-and-half, the remaining 2 tablespoons melted butter, and the confectioners' sugar in a bowl until smooth. Drizzle the sauce over the warm pudding before serving.

DESSERTS:

HAPPY DANCE WORTHY

Nothing brings more smiles to the table than a homemade dessert. Nothing makes the cook happier than creating those desserts quickly using supermarket shortcuts.

Use a cake mix to bake ginger-and-nutmeg-scented Spice Cookies. For Strawberry Shortcakes, refrigerated biscuits are sprinkled with sugar, baked, split, and layered with strawberry jam compote. Peach Crumb Bars come together in no time with a filling of puréed dried peaches and peach jam.

These recipes are so easy that your kids can measure, mix, and pour right along with you. They will be proudly grinning from ear to ear when offering a plate of David's Oversized Chocolate Chunk Cookies. The Snickerdoodle Mug Cake is a one-serving wonder that they'll beg to make. For the Piña Colada Cake, let them poke holes with the round end of a wooden spoon into the baked pound cake and watch as the coconut milk and pineapple juice are absorbed. Lemon Snacking Cake is easy to measure and mix by hand—perfect for young aspiring bakers.

Get out your bowls and spoons and warm up your happy dance.

Peach Crumb Bars

Dried rather than frozen fruit combined with preserves keeps these golden fruit bars from becoming soggy. While peaches and peach preserves are used here, try whatever you have in your pantry. Pair dried raspberries, apricots, mango, or cherries with matching preserves. Once cooled and cut, wrap them individually and freeze.

MAKES 18

Vegetable oil spray

2 4-ounce bags **dried sliced peaches**

1 18-ounce jar **peach preserves**

½ teaspoon ground nutmeg

2 cups (4 sticks) unsalted butter, at room temperature

1 tablespoon pure vanilla extract

3¾ cups all-purpose flour

1 cup sugar

1 teaspoon table salt

Heat the oven to 350°F. Lightly coat the bottom of a 9 x 13-inch baking pan with vegetable oil spray. Line the bottom and two sides of the baking pan with a piece of parchment paper. Lightly coat the paper with vegetable oil spray. Set aside.

Put the peach slices, peach preserves, and nutmeg in a food processor and process until the fruit is finely chopped. Set aside.

Put the butter and vanilla in the bowl of an electric mixer. Beat on high speed until creamy. Reduce the speed to low and add the flour, sugar, and salt until it has a crumbly, coarse texture. Do not overmix.

Press half of the dough mixture into the prepared pan. Spread the peach mixture evenly on top. Using your fingers, evenly sprinkle the remaining crumbly dough over the peach layer.

Bake for 60 to 65 minutes, until the top is light golden brown. Remove the pan from the oven and let cool completely on a wire rack before cutting into bars.

David's Oversized Chocolate Chunk Cookies

When you sink your teeth into these soft cookies, you get big, bold bites of milk chocolate goodness. Golden brown around the edges and gooey inside, these cookies are so big that you need two sheet pans to make them. These are the best cookies ever.

MAKES 10 COOKIES

1½ cups all-purpose flour

½ teaspoon baking powder

½ teaspoon kosher salt

⅛ teaspoon baking soda

7 tablespoons unsalted butter, at room temperature

½ cup (packed) light brown sugar

¼ cup granulated sugar

1 tablespoon pure vanilla extract

1 large egg

3 4.4-ounce or 2 7-ounce bars Hershey's milk chocolate, broken into ½- to ¾-inch pieces

Heat the oven to 350°F. Line two sheet pans with parchment paper.

Whisk together the flour, baking powder, salt, and baking soda in a bowl and set aside.

Put the butter, both sugars, and vanilla in the bowl of an electric mixer. Beat on high speed until creamy, 2 to 3 minutes. Add the egg and beat until combined. Reduce the speed to medium-low, add the flour mixture, and mix until a dough forms. Stir in the chocolate pieces. Using an ice cream scoop, scoop the dough into ¼-cup balls and place 5 on each prepared sheet pan about 2½ inches apart. Don't flatten the balls. Refrigerate the cookies for 10 to 12 minutes—no longer—so they don't spread.

Remove the cookies from the refrigerator and bake until the cookies are puffed with light golden-brown edges, 16 to 18 minutes. Cool on a wire rack.

Spice Cookies

Make these cookies once and you'll be sure to keep a spice cake mix on hand for those times when you must have something sweet. Thanks to the mix, these treats are soft, chewy, and cakey on the inside with a warm, brown-sugary coating. I like them with a cup or two of strong coffee.

MAKES 20 COOKIES

1 15.25-ounce **spice cake mix**

⅓ cup vegetable oil

2 large eggs

1 teaspoon plus ½ teaspoon **pumpkin pie spice**

⅓ cup (packed) light brown sugar

Heat the oven to 350°F. Line two sheet pans with parchment paper.

Put the cake mix, oil, eggs, and 1 teaspoon pumpkin pie spice in the bowl of an electric mixer. Beat on medium speed until a sticky dough forms, about 1 minute. Set aside.

Mix together the brown sugar and the remaining ½ teaspoon pumpkin pie spice in a shallow bowl.

Using a mini ice cream scoop, spoon 2 tablespoons of cookie dough into the bowl with the sugar-spice mixture and gently roll it to coat. Repeat with the remaining dough. Place the cookies 2 inches apart on the prepared sheet pans.

Bake the cookies, rotating the pans halfway through the baking time, until puffed and cracked, 12 to 14 minutes. Remove from the oven and place the sheet pans on a cooling rack. Let the cookies cool before serving.

Apple Cake

The simple name of this cake doesn't do it justice. Rich, dense, and moist, it's made with oil rather than butter and packed with lots of apple flavor. Trust me, you'll be making this delightful dessert frequently. Serve with cups of Masala Chai Lattes (page 233) on a brisk afternoon by the fire.

A couple of tips: Make this in a 10-inch standard Bundt pan; a fancy pan with lots of nooks won't release the cake properly. And prepare the apples after the batter is made, not before.

This cake keeps well and, like many baked goods, it's so much better the next day.

MAKES 12 SERVINGS

1 cup vegetable oil, plus more for the pan

2 cups all-purpose flour, plus more for the pan

2 teaspoons baking powder

½ teaspoon table salt

1⅓ cups plus ⅓ cup plus 2 tablespoons sugar

1½ tablespoons plus 1½ teaspoons ground cinnamon

3 large eggs

2 teaspoons pure vanilla extract

4 cups peeled, cored, and cut ½-inch cubes Granny Smith apples
(*Use no more than 26 ounces before they are prepped and 17 to 19 ounces once cubed.*)

Heat the oven to 350°F. Grease and flour a 10-inch Bundt pan.

Whisk the flour, baking powder, and salt together in a bowl and set aside. Put the oil, 1⅓ cups sugar, the eggs, and vanilla in the bowl of an electric mixer. Beat on high speed until thick and light yellow in color, about 4 minutes. On low speed, add the dry ingredients and mix just until combined.

Toss the apples in a bowl with ⅓ cup sugar and 1½ tablespoons cinnamon.

Pour half of the cake batter into the prepared pan, then spoon half of the apple mixture over it. Pour the remaining cake batter and top with the other half of the apple mixture. Combine the remaining 2 tablespoons sugar with the remaining 1½ teaspoons cinnamon and sprinkle on top.

Bake until a toothpick inserted in several places comes out clean, 70 to 80 minutes. Remove from the oven and let cool on a wire rack for 45 minutes. Invert cake onto a pan and immediately flip back onto a serving plate and let cool completely.

Piña Colada Cake

Turn a favorite tropical cocktail into a refreshing dessert. Poke holes all over a pound cake made with a mix, then pour on a blend of pineapple juice and coconut milk. Spoon on crushed pineapple, then spread the cake with a smooth whipped-cream topping and sprinkles of shredded coconut.

MAKES 12 TO 15 SERVINGS

Vegetable cooking spray

1 15-ounce box **pound cake mix**

1 13.5-ounce can **coconut milk**

1½ cups canned **pineapple juice**

1 8-ounce can **crushed pineapple**

¾ cup toasted **shredded coconut**

1¾ cups heavy cream

⅓ cup confectioners' sugar

1 tablespoon coconut extract

Coat a 9 × 13-inch baking pan with vegetable cooking spray. Prepare the pound cake mix according to package instructions. Pour it into the prepared pan and bake until light golden brown on top and a toothpick inserted in several places comes out clean, 34 to 36 minutes. Allow the cake to cool for 15 minutes.

Whisk together the coconut milk and pineapple juice in a bowl. Using the round end of a wooden spoon, evenly poke holes all over and through the cake to the pan. Evenly pour the coconut milk–pineapple juice over the cake. Evenly spoon the crushed pineapple on top. Let the still-warm cake cool on a wire rack for 35 minutes. Cover with plastic wrap and refrigerate for at least 3 hours or overnight.

Put the heavy cream, confectioners' sugar, and coconut extract in the bowl of an electric mixer. Beat on medium-high speed until medium peaks form, about 4 minutes. Spread the whipped cream all over the cake. Garnish with the toasted coconut before slicing and serving.

Strawberry Shortcakes

Talk about a dessert that is half homemade yet fully delicious! This classic summer dessert is easy to put together with refrigerated biscuits. The biscuit halves are piled with cooked strawberries and a whipped-cream filling thickened with cheesecake-flavored instant pudding. Sparkling sugar adds a sweet and glittery touch to each serving.

MAKES 8 SERVINGS

1 pound plus 1 pound fresh strawberries, stemmed and quartered

⅔ cup granulated sugar

1 16.3-ounce can **Pillsbury Grands! Southern Homestyle biscuits**

2 tablespoons unsalted butter, melted

3 tablespoons white sparkling sugar

3 cups heavy cream

1 1-ounce package **sugar-free fat-free cheesecake flavor instant pudding mix**

1 tablespoon pure vanilla extract

Combine 1 pound strawberries and the granulated sugar in a saucepan and let sit for 10 minutes. Bring the strawberries to a boil, then immediately reduce the heat to medium. Cook, stirring frequently, until the strawberries break down and the mixture is thick, 25 to 30 minutes. Remove the saucepan from the heat and let the mixture cool completely. Fold in the remaining 1 pound strawberries, cover, and refrigerate until needed.

Heat the oven to 375°F. Line a sheet pan with parchment paper.

Separate the biscuits into 8 pieces. Dip one side of each biscuit into the melted butter and arrange them on the prepared sheet pan. Sprinkle each with the sparkling sugar. Bake until light brown around the edges, 12 to 14 minutes. Let cool completely on a wire rack.

Put the heavy cream, pudding mix, and vanilla in the bowl of an electric mixer. Beat on medium-high speed until stiff peaks form, about 2 minutes.

Cut the biscuits in half through the middle (16 halves). Layer 8 of the biscuits with some of the whipped cream and some of the strawberry filling. Place the remaining biscuits on top. Spoon a dollop of the whipped cream next to each shortcake and top with the remaining strawberry filling before serving.

Lemon Snacking Cake

When I want something sweet and I want it quickly, this easy-to-put-together treat does the trick. Mix everything up, pour it into a pan, and, in just over a half hour, the result is a super-moist dessert. It combines the best of lemon cake and lemon bars in one scrumptious treat. Have a square. Or maybe two?

MAKES 9 SERVINGS

Vegetable oil spray

2 cups cake flour, sifted

1 teaspoon baking powder

½ teaspoon table salt

¼ teaspoon baking soda

1⅓ cups sugar

Juice and zest of 3 large lemons

½ cup vegetable oil

1 large egg plus 2 large egg yolks

¾ cup sour cream

Heat the oven to 350°F. Lightly coat the bottom of a 9 × 9-inch baking pan with vegetable oil spray. Line the bottom and two sides of the baking pan with a piece of parchment paper. Lightly coat the paper with the vegetable oil spray.

Whisk the cake flour, baking powder, salt, and baking soda together in a bowl. Set aside.

Stir together the sugar and lemon zest in a separate bowl until the zest is well coated with the sugar. Whisk in the oil, egg, and egg yolks until well combined. Whisk in the sour cream, then fold in the flour mixture, alternating with the lemon juice until incorporated. Do not overmix. Pour the batter evenly into the prepared pan.

Bake until a toothpick inserted in several places comes out clean, 30 to 35 minutes. Remove the pan from the oven and let cool on a wire rack for 20 minutes. Invert the cake onto a cutting board, remove the parchment paper, and immediately flip the cake back onto a serving plate. Let cool completely before cutting. Store in an airtight container up to 4 days.

Snickerdoodle Mug Cake

What more could you ask for? A single-serving cake that is mixed and microwaved in a 10- to 12-ounce straight-sided mug. Oh, did I mention all the cinnamony, snickerdoodley cookie deliciousness in each cup? Your young bakers will beg to make this individual treat. I imagine some older folks will, too.

MAKES 1 SERVING

⅓ cup all-purpose flour

2 tablespoons plus 1½ teaspoons sugar

¼ teaspoon baking powder

Pinch of table salt

¼ cup milk

3 tablespoons unsalted butter, melted

¾ teaspoon pure vanilla extract

¼ teaspoon ground cinnamon

Using a fork, whisk together the flour, 2 tablespoons sugar, baking powder, and salt in a 10- to 12-ounce microwave-safe mug. Stir in the milk, butter, and vanilla until combined, making sure to scrape well all around the mug. Let sit for 1 minute.

Combine the remaining 1½ teaspoons sugar with the cinnamon in a bowl. Sprinkle over the top of the cake batter. Microwave for 1 minute 45 seconds, until the cake is set and firm to the touch. Allow to cool for 3 to 5 minutes before digging in with a spoon.

Banana-Caramel Pie

Banana lovers, go no further. You have found your pie. Refrigerated pie crust is baked and layered with canned dulce de leche, a Latin American caramel sauce, and sliced bananas. Once chilled, a blizzard of whipped cream is spread on top and then garnished with chopped walnuts. When sliced, each layer in this stacked masterpiece stands out. When eaten, each bite is a burst of individual flavors that meld together perfectly.

MAKES 8 SERVINGS

1 refrigerated **pie crust**

¼ cup plus 1 cup canned **dulce de leche**

3 tablespoons plus 1⅓ cups heavy cream

3 ripe bananas, sliced into ¼-inch pieces

2 tablespoons **white chocolate instant pudding mix**

1½ teaspoons pure vanilla extract

3 tablespoons chopped walnuts, toasted

Bake the pie crust in a 9-inch pie plate following the package instructions for a one-crust baked shell. Let cool completely.

Whisk together ¼ cup dulce de leche and 3 tablespoons heavy cream in a bowl and refrigerate until needed.

Gently spread the remaining 1 cup dulce de leche over the cooled crust. Arrange the banana slices on top. Put the remaining 1 ⅓ cups heavy cream, the instant pudding, and vanilla in the bowl of an electric mixer. Beat on medium-high speed until stiff peaks form, about 2 minutes. Spoon the whipped cream evenly over the pie and spread until bananas are completely covered.

Refrigerate for 2 hours. Sprinkle on the chopped walnuts. Drizzle on the refrigerated caramel sauce before slicing and serving.

Chocolate Dream Icebox Pie

Mom kept frozen chocolate cream pies on hand to cool us off on hot summer days. I had my own particular way of enjoying them: Start with the whipped cream rosettes, followed by the filling, and then eat the pastry crust. This no-bake pie captures those memorable flavors. A creamy chocolate-cheesecake filling is spread in a ready-made Oreo cookie pie crust. Once chilled, pile on the whipped topping and garnish with chocolate shavings.

MAKES 8 SERVINGS

1⅔ cups milk chocolate chips

⅓ cup light cream

1 teaspoon **instant espresso coffee granules**

1 8-ounce package cream cheese, at room temperature

¼ cup sugar

1½ teaspoons pure vanilla extract

1 8-ounce container **Cool Whip**, divided into 1 cup and 2 cups, chilled

1 8-inch (6-ounce) **Oreo Pie Crust**

Chocolate shavings

Put the chocolate chips, light cream, and instant espresso in a microwave-safe bowl. Microwave for 40 seconds at a time, stirring between each interval, until the chocolate is melted. Set aside to cool.

Put the cream cheese, sugar, and vanilla in the bowl of an electric mixer. Beat on medium-high speed until creamy, about 2 minutes. Add the cooled chocolate mixture and continue beating until the mixture is smooth and evenly combined. Add 1 cup of the whipped topping and mix until fully incorporated.

Evenly spread the chocolate filling into the pie crust. Evenly spread the remaining 2 cups whipped topping over the pie. Refrigerate for 8 hours or overnight. Serve each slice with a garnish of chocolate curls on top.

DRINKS:

RAISE YOUR GLASSES

Share your flair for the dramatic by adding elegant touches and standout garnishes to cocktails and other drinks. How you present drinks is just as important as how they taste. Choose the right glass for each drink. Pair drinks with appropriate garnishes like citrus twists, melon balls on skewers, or herb sprigs. Presentation does make a difference.

Offer guests bright pink Chocolate-Cherry Martinis in glasses dipped in chocolate syrup and shavings. Cool off with Mango Lassis, a cooling, creamy blend of frozen mango and yogurt. As soon as spring arrives, rosé wines ranging in color from pale pink to soft peach to muted strawberry are stacked up in wine shops. Instead of the usual white-wine-and-club-soda spritzers, Rosé Summer Spritzers combine dry rosé wine with muddled strawberries, grenadine syrup, and ginger ale for a cool, refreshing beverage. Serve awesome, all-in-one Banana Split Milkshakes in the tallest glasses you own.

Spiced Coffee-Cookie Shakes

Lotus Biscoff cookies, made in Belgium, are a delightful blend of sugar and spices. In this coffee drink, some of the cookies are blended with a double dose of coffee, ice cream, and warming spices. Each glass of this grown-up beverage receives a spritz of whipped cream, a drizzle of caramel sauce, and an extra cookie. The result is an after-dinner treat that combines the best of coffee and dessert.

MAKES 4 SERVINGS

2½ cups strong brewed coffee, chilled

2 cups vanilla ice cream

2 teaspoons **gingerbread spice**

2 teaspoons **instant espresso coffee granules**

¼ teaspoon ground cloves

10 plus 4 **Lotus Biscoff cookies**

Canned whipped cream

½ cup **caramel syrup**

Put the coffee, ice cream, gingerbread spice, instant espresso, cloves, 10 cookies, and 2 cups ice into a blender. Blend until smooth, 60 to 70 seconds.

Divide the mixture among four tall glasses. Top each with a squirt of whipped cream and 1 of the remaining cookies. Add a drizzle of caramel sauce to each one before serving.

Masala Chai Lattes

Chai means "tea" in many languages. In India, chai is black tea with milk. For masala chai, warm, comforting spices, like cinnamon and nutmeg are added. Serve cups of this soothing beverage on chilly afternoons with a plate of cookies. Don't forget to add a healthy dollop of whipped cream on top.

MAKES 4 SERVINGS

4 cups vanilla almond milk

2 teaspoons ground cinnamon

1 teaspoon ground ginger

½ teaspoon ground nutmeg

1 star anise

5 black or English breakfast tea bags

2 tablespoons honey

2 tablespoons (packed) light brown sugar

Canned whipped cream

Ground allspice

Heat the almond milk, cinnamon, ginger, nutmeg, and star anise in a saucepan. As soon as the mixture starts to boil, turn off the heat. Immediately add the tea bags and steep for 6 to 8 minutes.

Remove the tea bags and the star anise. Turn on the heat to medium and stir in the honey and brown sugar. Cook, stirring constantly, until the mixture is hot and the sugar dissolves. Divide the mixture among four cups. Top each serving with some whipped cream and a dash of allspice.

Mango Lassis

A lassi, a creamy, cooling yogurt-based drink from the Indian subcontinent, is served with or after a meal. Here, yogurt and frozen mango are blended until smooth. I serve these refreshing palate cleansers on warm summer evenings after enjoying platters of barbecue or take-out Indian food. Enjoy them anytime of the day, and feel free to improvise with frozen pineapple, bananas, strawberries, or other fruit.

MAKES 4 SERVINGS

1 14-ounce package **frozen mango pulp**, thawed

½ cup whole milk

2 tablespoons honey

1 cup plain Greek yogurt

¼ teaspoon plus ⅛ teaspoon ground nutmeg

⅛ teaspoon plus ⅛ teaspoon ground cinnamon

1½ cups **frozen mango chunks**

Put 1 cup water, the thawed mango pulp, milk, honey, yogurt, ¼ teaspoon nutmeg, ⅛ teaspoon cinnamon, and the frozen mango chunks into a blender. Blend until smooth, thick, and creamy, about 60 seconds.

Divide the lassi among four glasses and sprinkle the remaining ⅛ teaspoon nutmeg and ⅛ teaspoon cinnamon on top of each drink.

Banana Split Milkshakes

I love old-fashioned soda fountain drinks and other ice-cream concoctions, so I decided to combine the ingredients of my two favorites—a banana split and a milkshake—into one drink. Each tall glass is topped with some fluffy whipped cream, caramel and chocolate sauces, chopped nuts, and—the crowning touch—a bright red cherry. You can drink this with a straw, but you'll also want a spoon to get every bit of creamy goodness from the glass.

MAKES 4 SERVINGS

2⅔ cups strawberry ice cream

3 ripe bananas

2 cups whole milk

⅓ cup semisweet mini chocolate chips

¼ cup plus 4 tablespoons canned **crushed pineapple**

Canned whipped cream

½ cup **caramel syrup**

½ cup **chocolate sauce**

¼ cup toasted and chopped walnuts

4 maraschino cherries

Put the ice cream, bananas, milk, chocolate chips, and ¼ cup crushed pineapple into a blender. Blend until smooth, about 90 seconds.

Divide the milkshake among four tall glasses and top each one with some whipped cream. Garnish each drink with some of the caramel syrup, chocolate sauce, walnuts, and crushed pineapple. Finish with a maraschino cherry on top.

Rosé Summer Spritzers

Here's a "pitcher perfect" warm-weather thirst quencher. Strawberries are muddled and combined with a bottle of rosé wine and grenadine syrup. Before serving, pour in some ginger ale for just the right amount of bubbly zip. Serve these cocktails to your guests while waiting for the grill to heat up.

MAKES 6 TO 8 SERVINGS

1½ cups stemmed and quartered strawberries

1 (750 ml) bottle dry rosé wine, chilled

1 cup grenadine

3 cups ginger ale, chilled

1 lemon, ends trimmed and cut into 6 to 8 slices

Fresh mint sprigs

Put the strawberries in a large pitcher and, using a wooden spoon, gently muddle the strawberries until mashed. Add the wine and grenadine, stirring well to combine. Cover and refrigerate until needed.

Just before serving, stir the ginger ale into the pitcher. Pour the spritzer mix into glasses filled with ice. Garnish each drink with a slice of lemon and a sprig of mint.

Orange Crush

For more than two decades, I've spent lots of time along the Delaware shore, where every bar and restaurant serves this summery cocktail. Orange juice, vodka, and orange-flavored liqueur are shaken together and poured into a tall glass over ice. Instead of making individual drinks, I combine all the ingredients in a pitcher. Right before serving, I stir in lemon-lime soda. The beach just came to your backyard.

MAKES 4 SERVINGS

1½ cups fresh orange juice

1 cup lemon-lime soda

½ cup orange-flavored vodka

½ cup orange liqueur, such as triple sec or Grand Marnier

4 mint sprigs

4 orange wedges

Pour the orange juice, soda, vodka, and orange liqueur into a pitcher and stir well.

Fill four tall glasses with crushed ice and pour in the mixture. Garnish each glass with a mint sprig and an orange wedge.

Chocolate-Cherry Martinis

Chocolate-covered cherries, also called cordials, were a Christmastime treat for us kids: A cherry is encased in a chocolate shell along with a cherry-flavored syrup. Turn that same chocolaty-cherryliciousness into a cocktail with flavored vodkas and crème de cacao. Pour this pink drink into chocolate-rimmed glasses and serve at winter holiday parties or on Valentine's Day.

MAKES 4 SERVINGS

Chocolate sauce

¼ cup thin **chocolate shavings**

16 stemmed **maraschino cherries**
and ¼ cup syrup from the jar

¾ cup chocolate vodka

½ cup cherry vodka

¼ cup crème de cacao

¼ cup light cream

To decorate the glasses, pour the chocolate syrup on one plate and put the chocolate shavings on another. Dip the rims of each martini glass into the chocolate syrup, then the shaved chocolate to coat all around. (The glasses can be decorated and refrigerated ahead of time.) Skewer 4 cherries each on four cocktail toothpicks.

To make 1 martini, put 1 cup ice, then 3 tablespoons chocolate vodka, 2 tablespoons cherry vodka, 1 tablespoon crème de cacao, 1 tablespoon cream, and 1 tablespoon cherry syrup in a cocktail shaker. Cover and shake well, until the outside of the shaker is frosty. Slowly strain the drink into the prepared glass. Repeat to make the other martinis, then garnish each glass with the cherries on toothpicks.

White Christmas Margaritas

No, you're not dreaming. Greet your holiday guests or end a festive meal with this wintry spin on a classic cocktail. The blended trifecta of tequila, coconut milk, and orange liqueur is perfect for your seasonal celebration. Garnish this very merry indulgence with lime slices, cranberries, and snowy coconut flakes.

MAKES 8 SERVINGS

1 13.5-ounce can **coconut milk**

1 cup coconut rum

1 cup coconut water

¾ cup orange liqueur, such as triple sec or Grand Marnier

¾ cup agave nectar

⅔ cup silver tequila

⅔ cup fresh lime juice

2 limes, cut into wedges and frozen

1 cup **frozen cranberries**

¼ cup sweetened coconut flakes

Coconut Milk

Coconut milk adds creaminess, richness, and a subtle coconut flavor to soups, curries, and desserts. It also whips up into a fine froth for latte toppings.

When you open a can of coconut milk, there will be a thick cream on top and a thinner liquid underneath. Shake the can well.

Canned coconut milk is thicker and preferable to the thin liquid in boxes. For savory recipes, be sure to use full-fat coconut milk, not cream of coconut, which is better suited for piña coladas and other cocktails.

Combine the coconut milk, coconut rum, coconut water, orange liqueur, agave, tequila, and lime juice in a blender. Blend on low speed until smooth, about 30 seconds. Refrigerate for at least 3 hours or overnight.

Just before serving, place a couple of frozen lime slices and a few frozen cranberries into each glass. Stir the margarita mixture well and divide it among eight glasses. Sprinkle coconut flakes in each glass before serving.

ACKNOWLEDGMENTS

I always begin with my dear family, particularly my precious mother, Sarah! From an early age you knew that teaching me to cook would benefit me my entire life and now it's my career! I love you with my whole heart.

To my close friends who are my extended family! First, big thanks to Jimmy D'Angelo, Cosmo and Dewey . . . your encouragement is so important to me. Also, Jane (Honey), Gail, Ed, Tara, Mikey, Jill, Lisa, and Joe. We have shared many meals together and I'm so grateful for each of you!

My *In The Kitchen with David* team: Melissa Gulli, my close friend, confidante, and fearless team leader. Big appreciation to Mary DeAngelis and Julia Cearley and your weekly focus on our show and the expertise and laughter you bring to both broadcasts. Ilana Bucholtz, my Wednesday producer and dear friend. You make me better and stronger—I adore you! Additional thanks to: Ed Kopania, Sean Hagan, Ray Radomicki, Marianne Shumbo, Tony LaBoy, Judy Mosteller, Carly Petitdemange, Elizabeth Malone, Liz Furlong, Heather Winters, Phil Falsone, Morgan Hart, Kelsey Brown, John Kehan, Lisa Guldin, Kim Kidd, Maureen Kelly, Megan Walters, Christy Mitchell, Patti D'Alesio, Maureen Siman, Katie Dougherty, and Alicia Rudd.

Special thanks to QVC culinary team members Chris Allen, Michele Pilone, and Jenn Teti for all of the cookbook chapter photography food styling.

Another big shout-out to all of our QVC culinary prep chefs who make our show so mouthwatering each week.

Anne Marie DiRocco, you are my saving grace. You keep my life on schedule and always ensure I am fully supported. I am lucky to have my schedule in your very capable hands!

Cookbook Project Manager Julie Hamilton, you are a driving force that kept the project moving smoothly from beginning to end.

My darling, Harriet Bell! To call you a friend doesn't begin to tell the story . . . you are FAMILY! Your words are my words and vice versa! We finish each other's sentences and I'm thankful for you every moment of every day!

Pamela Cannon, my editor at Penguin Random House. We've now produced four books together and I have such gratitude for you and everyone at Ballantine.

My photographer, Tina Rupp, you are a true artist. From the cover to the food photography . . . each shot tells a beautiful story. Special thanks go to Cyd McDowell for not only your incredible food styling skills, but also your humor. We are all a great team. I'll always remember our super fun Connecticut shoot!

Special thanks to Johanna Halsmith-Weisser for your incredible photography and to Wes Weisser for coordinating shoots, keeping me fed, and capturing behind-the-scenes content.

Huge thanks and congratulations to my culinary team of Stephen Delaney and Andrea Schwob. You took my concepts and made each one sing as well as taste incredible. You have the amazing ability to keep reworking a recipe until it is perfect! You both ROCK!

My creative director and team leader, Ana Tamaccio. You embraced this project with such joy and passion and I will always be grateful. Special thanks go to Senior Art Director Greg McDonnell, Content Designers Kelcey Hurst and Gabrielle Gorney, and finally, Senior Retouching Artists Pete Pfister and Elissa Tuerk.

My project and production team: Tom Ammon, Pat Sanborn, Carol Cotton, Kim Ent, and Shannon Whitmore. You all helped make the book special from page to page and chapter to chapter.

To our QVC management team: Mike George, Leslie Ferraro, Mary Campbell, Rob Robillard, Shannon Mallon, and Tim Bertoni. Many thanks for your support and encouragement. Special call out to Sue Schick, who not only provided me with plenty of cheerleading, but also secured a location for our team to test and retest all of the recipes.

To Christina Pennypacker, Mamey Roope, and Jessica Palek, my cookbook buyers. You are all wonderful collaborators and advocates.

Major callout for my stylist and friend Elisa DeVincenzi. You helped me shop online and build lots of outfits, so I could tell the story of the recipes and the cookbook. You are an angel!

To Iron Chef Geoffrey Zakarian for your friendship and mentorship. You are so wonderful to have written the foreword. I am very grateful that you found your way to QVC.

Finally, my biggest thanks go to our growing family of Foodies who watch *In the Kitchen with David* each week. Your enthusiasm for food and cooking continue to inspire me. All that I do on this show is for you. I'm forever grateful for your love, motivation, and encouragement. Our Foodies are the BEST!

INDEX

Note: Page numbers in *italics* indicate photos.

ABOUT THE AUTHOR

QVC's "resident foodie," **DAVID VENABLE** has been a program host since 1993 and has logged more than 12,000 hours in front of the camera. Viewers can watch him twice weekly on QVC's *In the Kitchen with David®* and anytime on his YouTube series, *Half Homemade*. Venable has appeared on NBC's *Today*, ABC's *The Chew*, the *Rachael Ray Show*, and Hallmark Channel's *Home & Family*. His recipes have been featured in *People, HuffPost, Woman's World*, and *Good Housekeeping*, as well as in other popular publications. Raised in North Carolina, Venable graduated from the University of North Carolina at Chapel Hill.

Facebook.com/DavidVenableQVC

Twitter: **@DavidVenableQVC**

Instagram: **@davidvenableqvc**

BY DAVID VENABLE

In the Kitchen with David:
QVC's Resident Foodie Presents
Comfort Foods That Take You Home

. . . .

In the Kitchen with David:
QVC's Resident Foodie Presents
Back Around the Table

. . . .

In the Kitchen with David:
QVC's Resident Foodie Presents
Comfort Food Shortcuts